Best Easy Day Hikes Series

Best Easy Day Hikes
Cape Cod and the Islands

Second Edition

Cheryl Johnson Huban
Updated by Pam VanDrimlen

FALCONGUIDES

GUILFORD, CONNECTICUT
HELENA, MONTANA
AN IMPRINT OF GLOBE PEQUOT PRESS

FALCONGUIDES®

Copyright © 1999, 2011 by Morris Book Publishing, LLC

FalconGuides is an imprint of Globe Pequot Press.
Falcon, FalconGuides, and Outfit Your Mind are registered trademarks of Morris Book Publishing, LLC.

Project editor: Gregory Hyman
Layout: Kevin Mak
Maps: Trailhead Graphics Inc. © Morris Book Publishing, LLC

TOPO! Explorer software and SuperQuad source maps courtesy of National Geographic Maps. For information about TOPO! Explorer, TOPO!, and Nat Geo Maps products, go to www.topo.com or www.natgeomaps.com.

Library of Congress Cataloging-in-Publication Data is available on file.

ISBN 978-0-7627-6133-3

Printed in the United States of America

10 9 8 7 6 5 4 3 2 1

I would like to thank my family for helping me live my dream and all my friends who joined me on these wonderful hikes. I look forward to many more adventures!

—Pam VanDrimlen

Contents

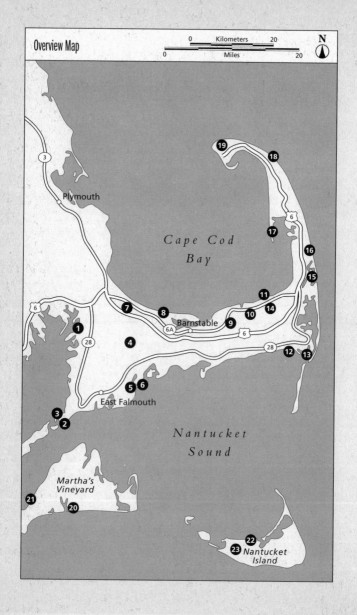

Kilometers

Miles

N

Plymouth

Cape Cod
Bay

Barnstable

East Falmouth

Nantucket
Sound

Martha's
Vineyard

Nantucket
Island

The Islands

Introduction

Cape Cod and the islands of Martha's Vineyard and Nantucket have become a summer paradise for millions of visitors each year. Shaped like an upraised arm, the Cape is riddled with Ice Age ponds and rimmed with wide expanses of white sand beaches. Birds and wildlife find homes in the salt and freshwater marshes that stretch beyond the defined waterways.

Ancient forests, quiet estuaries, and sandy dunes offer an escape from the hustle and bustle of a busy summer vacation or everyday life, as well as a glimpse of the Cape and Islands' varied terrain and historical past. This book is designed for those who wish to take the less-frequented road.

These hikes were selected from the many lovely spots on the Cape for their diversity and seclusion. Though they vary in length, most are 1 to 2 miles long, and the longest is 6.2 miles round-trip. All hikes are on easy-to-follow trails, and you can reach all trailheads in a regular passenger car.

Some of the hikes in this book will challenge the physically fit, others are easy enough for young children, and some are accessible to people with disabilities (depending on the weather). The Cape and the Islands are relatively flat; the majority of hikes have only minor changes in elevation, and the largest climb gains a total of 158 feet.

To help you decide on the right trail, the trails are ranked from easiest to most challenging. Please keep in mind that long does not always equal difficult. Other factors, such as elevation gain, soft sand, and other trail conditions, have to be considered. To approximate how long it will take you to complete a given trail, use the standard of

2 miles per hour, adding time if you are not a strong hiker or are traveling with small children, and subtracting time if you are in good shape. Add time for picnics, rest stops, or other activities you plan for your outing.

Detailed maps may be available at some of the trailheads, and the pertinent USGS topographical map is listed with each hike. Unfortunately, the USGS maps are dated, and many of the hikes are not shown, but general location and direction are noted.

I hope you thoroughly enjoy your "best easy" hiking journey through the natural wonders of Cape Cod and the Islands!

The Nature of Cape Cod and the Islands

Most of the conservation areas on Cape Cod and the Islands are flat with small hills. The deep sand can be quite a workout, and you must always watch for tidal flows along ocean hikes. Although you won't find a diverse range of topography, the views and wildlife are the reward for visiting the area.

Weather
Cape weather could best be described as moderate New England. New England winters can be harsh and springs rainy and gloomy. Whatever the weather is in most of the state, it will be a bit less severe here.

Spring and fall are generally the most enjoyable time to walk the trails on Cape Cod and the Islands. You will generally not have to fight for parking and may not see anything other than nature for hours.

The signs of spring boast native birds and critters scooting around foraging for food. Hikers may find that the rains can be persistent, and some trails will flood or get quite muddy. Although many spring days will be unseasonably warm, it is mostly cool—in the 40s and 50s until late May.

Fall brings gorgeous foliage and red carpets of color as the cranberry bogs ripen before harvesting. The weather is usually ideal on the Cape until November. It seems the sun is more plentiful than rain or fog. The mercury doesn't fall much from 70 degrees, the air is crisp, and the sky is a clear striking blue. Fall is the ideal season for a best easy day hike.

Most visitors arrive in the summertime. Although the parking can become a challenge and the roads are busy, you can find solace on the trails. Summer brings the roasting sun, but most trails are blessed with beautiful tall trees to shade your hike. When the weatherman is predicting hot and humid, you can rest easy knowing that the Cape Cod breezes will keep the peninsula about 10 degrees cooler than the rest of the state.

Winter is a beautiful time to enjoy the hikes without the crowds; however, you need to watch for ice on many trails as they are shaded, and be sure to watch for alerts of parking lots that are seasonal and not accessible in winter.

Critters

Cape Cod is home to many harmless creatures. The deer, coyotes, squirrels, wild turkey, raccoons, opossums, rabbits, and many other small animals share in the glory of these wonderfully preserved sites. Many you will not see, but if you have a quick eye, you might catch a glimpse. The conservation commissions ask that you do not feed any wildlife and just enjoy their habitat with them. More good news: There are no poisonous snakes on the Cape.

Bird-watching is a popular pastime on Cape Cod. You can find an abundance of guidebooks in the local shops and boutiques to help you identify the large variety of species. Be on the watch while in the marsh for tall wooden stands placed sporadically. These stands host the regal osprey making his nest up high on the platform atop the post.

Be Prepared

Only three real dangers exist on the Cape and the Islands: sun, poisonous plants, and insects. Be sure to pack a hat, sunglasses, suntan lotion—and then use them. Everyone wants a vacation tan, but if you overdo it, it can become a vacation disaster.

Familiarize yourself with the symptoms of heat-related conditions. Sunny, humid days are beautiful, but can cause heat stroke or heat exhaustion. The best way to avoid these afflictions is to wear clothing appropriate to the weather conditions, drink lots of water, and keep a pace that is within your physical limits.

The Cape is home to an abundance of wildlife and plant life. It's a beautiful world, but it also can be unpredictable. Keep your hands to yourself. Don't pick the flowers or finger foliage. Poison ivy comes in many varieties, from shrubs to trailing vines with leaves shiny or dull, green or red.

Be alert for ticks, especially in the spring and early summer. These tiny, flat, round parasites are less than ¼-inch long, and certain species have been associated with Lyme disease. Pack repellent for pesky mosquitoes and greenheads, the biting flies usually found in marshlands.

You'll enjoy hiking much more if you wear good socks and comfortable walking shoes. For a beach hike on soft sand, over-the-ankle boots or shoes add extra support.

Carry a backpack loaded with ample water or sport drink, snacks and/or a lunch, and a picnic ground cover. Add a bathing suit and towel if you are beach- or pond-bound.

Leave No Trace

Trails on Cape Cod and the Islands are heavily used year-round. We, as trail users and advocates, must be especially vigilant to make sure our passage leaves no lasting mark. Here are some basic guidelines for preserving trails in the region:

- Pack out all your own trash, including biodegradable items like orange peels. You might also pack out garbage left by less considerate hikers.

- Don't approach or feed any wild creatures—the ground squirrel eyeing your snack food is best able to survive if it remains self-reliant.

- Don't pick wildflowers or gather rocks, feathers, and other treasures along the trail. Removing these items will only take away from the next hiker's experience.

- Avoid damaging trailside soils and plants by remaining on the established route. This is also a good rule of thumb for avoiding poison ivy, a common regional trailside irritant.

- Don't cut switchbacks, which can promote erosion.

- Be courteous by not making loud noises while hiking.

- Many of these trails are multiuse, which means you'll share them with other hikers, trail runners, mountain bikers, and equestrians. Familiarize yourself with the proper trail etiquette, yielding the trail when appropriate.

- Use outhouses at trailheads or along the trail.

Land Management

The following government and private organizations manage most of the public lands described in this guide and can provide further information on these hikes and other trails in their service areas.

Bourne Conservation Trust; www.bourneconservation trust.org; 1104 Route 28A, Cataumet, MA 02534; (508) 563-2884

Falmouth Conservation Commission; www.300com mittee.org; 157 Locust Street, Falmouth, MA 02540; (508) 540-0876

Salt Pond Areas Bird Sanctuaries, Inc.; www.saltpond .info; P.O. Box 535, West Falmouth, MA 02574; (508) 548-8484

The Trustees of Reservations; www.thetrustees.org; 464 Abbott Avenue, Leominster, MA 01453; (978) 840-4446 x1914

Mashpee Conservation Commission; www.ci.mashpee .ma.us; 16 Great Neck Road North, Mashpee, MA 02649; (508) 539-1400

Barnstable Conservation Commission; www.town.barn stable.ma.us/conservation; 367 Main Street, Hyannis, MA 02601; (508) 862-4093

Green Briar Nature Center; www.thorntonburgess.org;

6 Discovery Hill Road, East Sandwich, MA 02537; (508) 888-6870

Yarmouth Department of Natural Resources; www .yarmouth.ma.us; 597 Forest Road, West Yarmouth, MA 02664; (508) 760-4800

Dennis Conservation Department; www.town.dennis .ma.us/dept/naturalres/natresources.htm; 485 Main Street, South Dennis, MA 02660; (508) 660-6123

Cape Cod Museum of Natural History; www.ccmnh.org; 869 Main Street, Brewster, MA 02631; (508) 896-3867

Chatham Planning Board; www.mychatham.com/hard ingsbeach; 483 Main Street, Chatham, MA 02633; (508) 945-5100

Monomoy National Wildlife Refuge; www.fws.gov/ northeast/monomoy; Wikis Way, Chatham, MA 02633; (508) 945-0594

Nickerson State Park; www.mass.gov/dcr/parks/south east/nick.htm; Route 6A, Brewster, MA 02631; (508) 896-3491

Cape Cod National Seashore; www.nps.gov/caco; 99 Marconi Site Road, Wellfleet, MA 02667; (508) 771-2144

Nantucket Conservation Commission; www.nantucket conservation.org; P.O. Box 13, Nantucket, MA 02554; (508) 228-2884

How to Use This Guide

This guide is designed to be simple and easy to use. Each hike is described with a map and summary information that delivers the trail's vital statistics including length, difficulty, fees and permits, park hours, canine compatibility, and trail contacts. Directions to the trailhead are also provided, along with a general description of what you'll see along the way. A detailed route finder (Miles and Directions) sets forth mileages between significant landmarks along the trail.

How the Hikes Were Chosen

This guide describes trails that are accessible to every hiker, whether visiting from out of town or a local resident. The hikes are no longer than 7 miles round-trip, and most are considerably shorter. They range in difficulty from flat excursions perfect for a family outing to more challenging treks. While these trails are among the best, keep in mind that nearby trails, sometimes in the same park or sometimes in a neighboring open space, may offer options better suited to your needs. Where applicable, alternatives are suggested in the Options section at the end of hike descriptions. I've selected hikes on Cape Cod and the neighboring islands, so wherever your starting point you'll find a great easy day hike nearby.

Selecting a Hike

These are all easy hikes, but easy is a relative term. Use the following difficulty ratings to choose a hike that is right for you and your hiking companions.

- **Easy** hikes are generally short and flat, taking no longer than an hour to complete.

- **Moderate** hikes involve increased distance and relatively mild changes in elevation, and will take one to two hours to complete.

- **Challenging** hikes feature some steep stretches, greater distances, and generally take longer than two hours to complete.

Keep in mind that what you think is easy is entirely dependent on your level of fitness and the adequacy of your gear (primarily shoes). Use the trail's length as a gauge of its relative difficulty—even if climbing is involved it won't be bad if the hike is less than 1 mile long. If you are hiking with a group, select a hike that's appropriate for the least fit and prepared in your party.

Approximate hiking times are based on the assumption that on flat ground, most walkers average 2 miles per hour. Adjust that rate by the steepness of the terrain and your level of fitness (subtract time if you're an aerobic animal and add time if you're hiking with kids), and you have a ballpark hiking duration. Be sure to add more time if you plan to picnic or take part in other activities like bird watching or photography.

Ranking the Hikes

The following list ranks the hikes in this book from easiest to most challenging.

Easiest

Most Challenging

★ Wheelchair/stroller accessible depending on the weather
° Marked for the visually impaired

Map Legend

Transportation

══⑥══	U.S. Highway
══⑥Ⓐ══	State Highway
─────	Local Road
═ ═ ═ ═	Unpaved Road

Trails

━ ━ ━ ━	Featured Trail
- - - - -	Trail
→	Direction of Route

Water/Land Features

⬭	Body of Water
∼∼	River/Creek
⸺ ⸺	Marsh/Bog
⁖⁖⁖	Sand

Symbols

═	Bench
⌣	Bridge
■	Building/Point of Interest
🗼	Lighthouse
▲	Mountain/Peak
🅿	Parking
🏕	Picnic Area
🖼	Scenic View
⚲	Spring
○	Town
⑫	Trailhead

The Upper Cape

The "Upper Cape" refers to the region of Cape Cod closest to the mainland. It includes the towns of Bourne, Falmouth, Sandwich, and Mashpee.

The Upper Cape was one of the first areas to be settled on the Cape, and each town has its own rich historical heritage. Natural resources were used to support agriculture, salt works, fishing, whaling, and glassworks. Remnants of this history are evident throughout the area and in the names of roads and villages. The Upper Cape also was blessed with farsighted citizens who donated acres of land to the public, all of which are waiting to be explored.

Gentle hills and fertile river basins support pitch pine forests and lush undergrowth. Interior forests of majestic hardwoods, including eastern red cedar and American holly, remain sole survivors of the original Cape landscape, having been spared from early settlers' needs for building materials. Defined by a manmade canal on the northwest, vast estuaries on the southwest, and sandy beaches on the north and south, the Upper Cape offers solitude for all those who seek it.

1 Red Brook Pond Conservation Area Trail

This is a delightful romp through pitch pine woods, along ridges with views of the forest and lush undergrowth—and best of all, a firsthand look at working cranberry bogs. The reserve is the perfect antidote for stress—the restful, cool woodlands offer a relaxing atmosphere for the casual hiker.

Distance: 1.2-mile lollipop
Approximate hiking time: 30 minutes
Difficulty: Easy, small rolling hills
Trail surface: Narrow, wooded, hard packed soil
Best season: Beautiful colors as bogs ripen during the fall season
Other trail users: None
Canine compatibility: Dog friendly

Fees and permits: None
Schedule: Dawn to dusk
Map: USGS Pocasset
Starting point: Thaxter Road, Bourne
Trail contact: Bourne Conservation Trust; www.bourne conservationtrust.org
Special considerations: Small parking area

Finding the trailhead: To reach the reserve from the Bourne Rotary, go south on MA 28 for 3.4 miles to Barlows Landing Road (look for sign for Pocasset/Wings Neck). Turn right and go for 1.8 miles, across County Road and under the railroad bridge to the stop sign. Turn left onto Shore Road. Go through the underpass, then go 0.2 mile to the small lot on the left at Thaxter Road. A sign on the corner reads RED BROOK POND CONSERVATION AREA. GPS N41 40.707'/W070 36.638'

The Hike

Beginning on a residential street, you will soon find the trailhead and enter into a canopy of trees to start the hike. Birds are plentiful; squirrels and rabbits frolic in the underbrush and an occasional deer wanders through the reserve. In the fall, the hardwood forest bursts into vibrant color, especially appealing against the red cranberries.

As you head onto the "south" trail, the bogs will come into view. One of the few fruits native to North America, cranberries grew wild on the Cape when the Pilgrims landed. These wild cranberry bogs were created when kettle ponds gradually filled up with silt and plant debris. The organic layers formed peat, and cranberry vines took root in the top layers of moss.

Native Americans used cranberries to color rugs and blankets, flavor pemmican cakes and succotash, and to treat wounds from poison arrows. Cranberries are rich in vitamin C, and whalers and pirates used them to prevent scurvy.

Miles and Directions

0.0 To begin the hike, walk east up Thaxter Road, left up the hill at the HIKING TRAILS sign. The trail is straight ahead, and is well marked with a map and signs on trees.

0.2 Turn right at the first trail intersection, walking onto the "middle" trail. Hike along the ridge, passing a huge, glacial boulder on the left.

0.6 Stay right at the Y intersection and descend to the first "south" trail. Turn left at the bog and follow its contours. Swing left onto the roadway to the second bog, turning right just before the bog begins. Stay on the road until you reach the trail at the end of the bog that heads back into the woods.

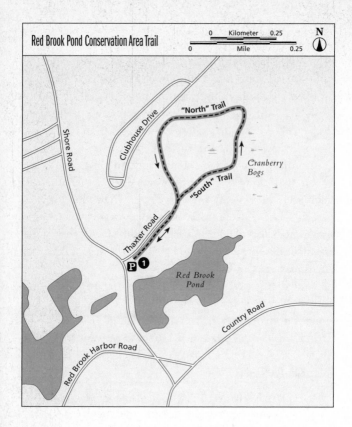

Red Brook Pond Conservation Area Trail

0　Kilometer　0.25
0　Mile　0.25

N

Clubhouse Drive

"North" Trail

Cranberry Bogs

"South" Trail

Shore Road

Thaxter Road

P **①**

Red Brook Pond

Country Road

Red Brook Harbor Road

0.8 Head back into the woods on the "north" trail. Climb the hill and turn left (west) at the top. Watch for animal prints on the sandy trail and catch glimpses of the bog below you on the left. The trail narrows through a section of new-growth pines, circling back to the trailhead.

1.2 Arrive back at the trailhead.

2 Beebe Woods

This is a great woodsy trail abundant with wildlife set behind the Cape Cod Conservatory, featuring a peaceful and serene forest to be enjoyed by all. Surrounded by several freshwater ponds, the trail is quite shaded and breezy. Check the schedule at the conservatory (www.capecodconservatory.org) and plan to take in a show after your hike.

Distance: 3.2 miles out and back

Approximate hiking time: 1.25 hours

Difficulty: Easy

Trail surface: Hard packed soil

Best season: All seasons

Other trail users: None

Canine compatibility: Dog friendly—keep leashed in parking lot

Fees and permits: None

Schedule: Dawn to dusk

Map: USGS Woods Hole

Starting point: 60 Highfield Drive, Falmouth

Trail contact: Falmouth Conservation Commission; www.300committee.org

Special considerations: Parking is at conservatory building

Finding the trailhead: To reach Beebe Woods from the Bourne Rotary, go south on MA 28 for 14 miles, through another rotary and past the spot where MA 28 turns into a two-lane road. Continue straight on Main Street when MA 28 veers off to the left into downtown Falmouth. (Follow the Woods Hole signs.) Turn right and go for 0.1 mile to the large white sign marking Depot Avenue. Continue for 0.5 mile to the end of Depot (aka Highfield Drive), driving behind the theater to the Cape Cod Conservatory parking area. GPS N41 33.518'/W070 37.783'

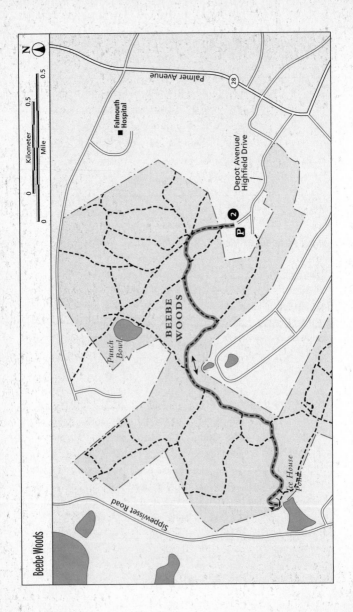

Beebe Woods

The Hike

This vast expanse of woodlands was donated by Mr. and Mrs. J. K. Lilly III to the town of Falmouth in 1976. Originally part of the summer estate of James M. Beebe, it is now bordered by residential areas. Carriage paths allow you to walk side by side, and dogs are welcome.

Swampy areas dot the woods, and a large pond is a serene destination. Glacial boulders sit as silent sentries, often surrounded by bearberry, bayberry, and blueberries.

Many trails bisect the 387 acres of woodland. Some are access for local homeowners, while others lead to kettle ponds or pass abandoned farm buildings. The narrow trails are marked by weathered signs and can be lengthier than they may appear at first. I recommend that you stay on the carriage paths unless you travel with a local guide.

Miles and Directions

0.0 The trail begins on the right (east side) of the conservatory building as you face it, and uphill to the left of the conservation sign. Enter the woods through an area of white pine into a clearing marked with a dramatic glacial boulder. Pass the boulder and turn left onto a wide sandy roadway. Stay on the carriage path.

0.2 While on the path, take the right fork.

0.4 Pass the Punch Bowl Trail and look for bearberry and bayberry, enjoying the cool shade. **Option:** Turn right (north) and make a visit to the Punch Bowl—a deep kettle pond (0.2-mile round-trip).

0.6 Reach the four corners. Stay on the pathway for 1.0 mile, ignoring the small trail intersections. At the fork, hook left. The trail narrows and curves around to Ice House Pond.

1.6 Walk down to Ice House Pond all the way to the metal fence and down to the waterline. Enjoy a rest at this peaceful spot, then return as you came.

3.2 Arrive back at the trailhead.

3 The Knob at Quissett Harbor Trail

This trail is unlike any other in this book. It is a wonderful way to see beautiful Quissett Bay with winding, wooded paths leading to "The Knob." This spit of land surrounded by water on three sides is small but so gorgeous it is definitely worth the trip.

Distance: 1.2-mile lollipop
Approximate hiking time: 40 minutes
Difficulty: Easy
Trail surface: Hard packed soil
Best season: Spring to fall. Watch for icy paths and wind in winter.
Other trail users: None
Canine compatibility: Dog friendly—not recommended in season

Fees and permits: None
Schedule: Dawn to dusk
Map: USGS Woods Hole
Starting point: Quissett Harbor Road, Falmouth
Trail contact: Salt Pond Areas Bird Sanctuaries, Inc.; www.salt pond.info
Special considerations: Narrow trails; parking in summer challenging

Finding the trailhead: To reach the start of The Knob trail from the Bourne Rotary, go south on MA 28 for 14 miles, through another rotary and past the spot where the route turns into a two-lane road. Continue straight on Main Street when MA 28 veers off to the left into downtown Falmouth. (Follow the Woods Hole signs.) At the stop sign (0.2 mile), turn right onto Locust Street. It is not marked. Stay on Locust for 1.7 miles to the stoplight at Quissett Harbor Road. Turn right and follow Quissett Harbor Road around the harbor to the far side. Limited parking is on the right, directly before the road ends on private property. GPS N41 32.684'/W070 39.353'

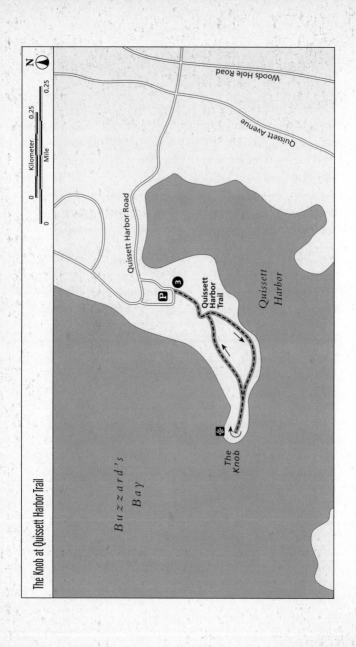

The Knob at Quissett Harbor Trail

N

0   0.25
Kilometer

0   0.25
Mile

Woods Hole Road

Quissett Avenue

Quissett Harbor Road

Quissett Harbor Trail

Quissett Harbor

The Knob

Buzzard's Bay

P

3

The Hike

This is a fun, scenic trail. It winds through woodlands past views of quaint Quissett Harbor to a child's paradise of ancient oak trees that invite climbing and are equipped with rope swings. Watch clammers patrol a rocky beach in search of dinner. Then, for the ultimate in pleasant hiking, walk up onto a rise above an intimate, rock-lined, crescent-shaped sandy beach and across a narrow causeway of coarse beach grass to "The Knob." This tiny round peninsula juts out into Buzzard's Bay and the view is spectacular.

To the far left, the Elizabeth Islands mound on the horizon. The towns of Wareham, Marion, Mattapoisett, and Fairhaven follow the coast from right to left. Sakonnet is the last town before the coast shifts around into Rhode Island Sound. A marble bench expresses the heartfelt thanks from all who visit to Cornelia L. Carey, who donated these thirteen acres of beauty at her death in 1973 to Salt Pond Areas Bird Sanctuaries, Inc.

Miles and Directions

0.0 Begin by crossing the road to the small entrance for the dirt trail, which leads up into the woods. Please stay on the cut trails at all times.

0.1 Turn left at the Y intersection and climb the steps. At the first trail intersection, turn right and follow the joyful sounds of children into a grove of magnificent oaks. Stay left, along the coastline, at each small trail intersection, until you reach a trail that descends to a rocky beach.

0.4 Stay along the shoreline trail. Choose the trail on the right and climb the slight rise. Walk back into the woods to a T intersection.

0.5 Walk back into the woods at the top of the loop where you turn left. On the right is a crescent-shaped beach, and you can catch glimpses of The Knob between the trees. Cross the causeway.

0.7 Climb steps to find the view from The Knob. Return the way you came to the trail intersection, then stay left (straight) to complete the loop and return to your car.

1.2 Arrive back at the trailhead.

4 Lowell Holly Reservation Trail

A great place for beachgoers and picnic lovers, this trail provides a wonderful setting to sit and relax beachfront on the pond and eat a delicious picnic lunch. This trail is frequented by dog lovers; feel free to bring your four-legged friend with you.

Distance: 3.8 miles out and back with a loop
Approximate hiking time: 1.5 hours
Difficulty: Easy/moderate
Trail surface: Hard packed soil
Best season: Spring to fall
Other trail users: None
Canine compatibility: Dog friendly—plenty of swimming
Fees and permits: None

Schedule: Dawn to dusk
Map: USGS Sandwich
Starting point: South Sandwich Road, Mashpee
Trail contact: The Trustees of Reservations; www.thetrustees .org
Special considerations: Icy paths in winter; parking lot fills quickly in summer

Finding the trailhead: To reach the Lowell Holly Reservation from US 6, exit 2, go south on MA 130 for 1.5 miles. Turn left on Cotuit Road and go for 3.5 miles. Turn right on South Sandwich Road for 0.6 mile to the parking lot on the right. GPS N41 39.9603'/W70 28.1799'

The Hike

This 135-acre peninsula divides Wakeby Pond and Mashpee Pond, two of the largest freshwater ponds on Cape Cod. A trail loop circles the two knolls of the peninsula, offering views of the lakes and a diversity of plant life.

Sweet gum, unique mosses, and ferns thrive here, along with the common day lily, which grows in the low spots.

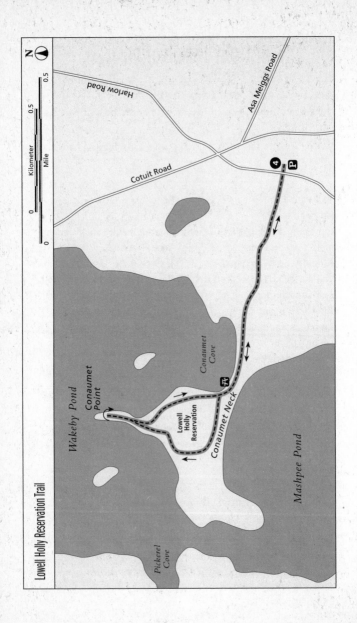

Lowell Holly Reservation Trail

Woodlands boast massive native American holly trees, stands of American beech, and red maples. Abbott Lawrence Lowell, longtime president of Harvard University, created this preserve as a private garden, enriching it with an array of other hardwoods and plants.

Miles and Directions

0.0 Start on the trail to the right of the information kiosk. Look below and to the left for glimpses of a freshwater marsh. Cross the manmade gully and continue through the forest. Ancient hollies intermingle with oaks, black birch, white birch, and pitch pine.

0.7 Reach the Wakeby shore and turn left. Pass two small beaches and climb through a grove of beech to a clearing. Turn left and follow the carriage path onto the peninsula. Stop to enjoy a picnic lunch at the clearing where tables allow for a lovely view of the pond.

0.9 Stay left at the Y intersection; begin the Overlook (Wheeler) Trail and follow the white squares. Turn left at the second trail intersection (red square).

1.2 Take the short walk over slightly elevated land, peeking through openings in the trees when you reach the Mashpee Pond overlook. Rejoin Overlook Trail and turn left (west). Watch for "turkey tails," a pore fungi, growing on downed trees.

1.8 Bear left (north) at the trail crossing at 1.8 miles, exploring Conaumet Point (marked by a blue square), a narrow spit of land dividing Mashpee and Wakeby Ponds.

2.7 Complete the loop. Return by retracing your steps past the small picnic area and up into the forest, returning to the trailhead.

3.8 Arrive back at the trailhead.

5 Long River Trail

Heavily wooded and hilly trails provide a great workout, complete with breathtaking views of the Mashpee River. This is one of the longer hikes in the book; take your time while sea birds pass overhead as you wind your way down the river.

Distance: 5.2-mile lollipop
Approximate hiking time: 2.25 hours
Difficulty: Moderate/challenging
Trail surface: Hard packed soil
Best season: Spring to fall
Other trail users: None
Canine compatibility: Dog friendly
Fees and permits: None
Schedule: Dawn to dusk

Map: USGS Cotuit
Starting point: Quinaquisset Avenue/Meetinghouse Road, Mashpee
Trail contact: Mashpee Conservation Commission; www.ci .mashpee.ma.us
Special considerations: Icy paths in winter; heavily wooded (watch for ticks)

Finding the trailhead: To reach the Mashpee River Woodlands from US 6, exit 2, go south on MA 130 for 7.5 miles. Turn right (south) onto Great Neck Road and drive for 2.2 miles to the Mashpee Rotary. Go around the rotary to MA 28, heading east to Hyannis. Go 0.4 mile to a right turn onto Quinaquissett Avenue and take an immediate right into the Mashpee River Woodlands North parking area. GPS N41 37.225'/W070 28.717'

The Hike

This hike takes you along the contours of hills rising above the 4-mile-long Mashpee River. Lined with tall cattails, the river bends several times, providing vistas that are unparalleled.

Conservation lands totaling 689 acres protect the undeveloped wooded shoreline and pristine river for nesting and migrating songbirds, hungry herons, and other native species. Listen for the calls of rufous-sided towhees and look for flickers, the only woodpeckers that feed on the ground.

The Mashpee River is one of the finest sea-run brook trout streams in Massachusetts. The best fishing is from the other bank of the river, which is also protected.

Miles and Directions

0.0 Depart from the left side of the information kiosk on the west side of the parking area. Follow the Long River Trail left (marked by a low 4x4 post etched with the initials of the trail—LR), through a small clearing. Pass a grove of azaleas and rhododendrons on your left as you descend toward the river, climbing up and scampering down the well-worn sandy trail through a hardwood forest.

0.6 Take the left fork at the trail intersection. Continue up and down, catching glimpses of the Mashpee River through the trees. Pass a towering pitch pine. The trail hooks left, dropping into a gully and returning to the river bluff. Take short detours on lookout trails for views of the river and marsh.

1.8 Reach Marsters Grove in a stand of pine on the right, giving tribute to the individual who sold 290 acres along the river to the Town of Mashpee. Stay riverside following the Chickadee Trail (CT). Private boat docks across the river indicate the boundary of the woodlands. Another trail marker points to the Partridge Berry Trail (PB). Stay on the Chickadee and continue into the depths of the woods.

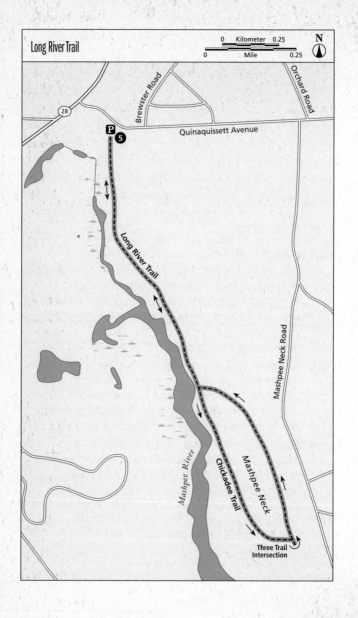

Long River Trail

Brewster Road

Orchard Road

28

Quinaquissett Avenue

P
5

Long River Trail

Mashpee Neck Road

Mashpee River

Chickadee Trail

Mashpee Neck

Three Trail
Intersection

Kilometer
0   0.25

Mile
0   0.25

N

2.6 Three trails intersect at an information kiosk near the Mashpee River Woodlands South parking area. Go left (north); the trail is not marked.

2.8 Reach the Whitcomb's Landing Trail (WL), turn left, and head back toward the river.

3.2 Rejoin the Long River Trail (LR) and retrace your steps to the parking area.

5.2 Arrive back at the trailhead.

6 Crocker Neck Conservation Area Trail

Located in Mashpee and surrounded by the picturesque Popponesset Bay, this easy hike has a small beach area and an observation deck to enjoy on Pinquickset Cove. It's fun for the whole family.

Distance: 2.2-mile lollipop
Approximate hiking time: 1 hour
Difficulty: Easy
Trail surface: Hard packed soil
Best season: Year-round
Other trail users: None
Canine compatibility: Dogs allowed (except on beach area 5/15–9/15)
Fees and permits: None

Schedule: Dawn to dusk
Map: USGS Cotuit
Starting point: Santuit Road, Barnstable
Trail contact: Barnstable Conservation Commission; www.town .barnstable.ma.us/conservation
Special considerations: Very small parking area

Finding the trailhead: To reach the Crocker Neck Conservation Area from the Mashpee Rotary, go east on MA 28 toward Hyannis for 0.4 mile. Turn right onto Quinaquissett Avenue. Continue southeast for 1.9 miles (the road turns into School Street just past the bay). Turn right (south) on Grove Street for 0.3 mile to its end at Santuit Road. Follow Santuit Road south for 0.7 mile, past Rushy Marsh Road, to the entrance on the left. The parking is very limited; you may have to continue south on Santuit around the bend for 0.3 mile to a narrow dirt road on the left. It is marked with a conservation sign, and a parking area is 0.1 mile farther down the dirt road. GPS N41 36.433'/W070 27.383'

The Hike

Bordered by water on two sides, this lovely ninety-seven-acre site was rescued from development in 1985. Named for the Crocker family, early settlers in the town of Barnstable, Crocker Neck includes woodland, salt marsh, freshwater marsh, shrub swamp, estuarine flats, and a small beach.

Markers call attention to some of the unique features of the area. The lower 1.0-mile loop is easy walking, although some of the trail is soft sand. The upper trail is slightly hilly, with native holly dotting the landscape of pine and oak woods. Underbrush of blueberry and huckleberry form a knee-high green hedge.

An observation deck is the perfect vantage point from which to watch herons or catch a glimpse of a great horned owl. Look for tiny minnows in the water or catch fiddler crabs before they dart into their burrows. Bring a picnic to enjoy at the observation deck or beach area.

Miles and Directions

0.0 The trail begins at the large sign on Santuit Road. (If you parked in the lot down the dirt road, you'll start by passing through a gray gate to marker 6.) Pass the gate and walk southeast on the sandy path.

0.3 Pass a clearing—probably a century-old sand barrow pit. Walk through the clearing to the southeast corner and follow the narrow trail across the dike into the marsh and marker 4. Return to the clearing and cross it to the southwest corner, picking up the narrow trail into the woods on the right. Pass marker 5. At the fork turn left.

0.6 The narrow trail ends. Make a sharp left and walk south. (If you've started at the second lot, pass through the gray

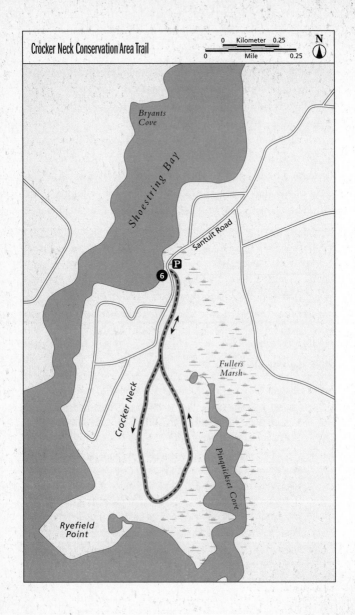

Crocker Neck Conservation Area Trail

gate.) Marker 6 draws attention to black huckleberry bushes. A small trail on the right leads into a stand of white pine. Return to the main trail.

0.8 The main trail ends in a circle. The narrow trail on the right takes you to a small bog. On the left is a picnic area and a beautiful view of Pinquickset Cove. Continue on the trail at the south end of the circle to the observation deck. Watch carefully for the osprey family, then follow the trail 0.1 mile south to a small sandy clearing.

0.9 Descend to the small wading beach. After you've rested on the beach, take the left trail straight north to the parking area.

1.3 Return to the parking area. You'll arc sharply right toward the gray gate; at marker 6, make a sharp left and retrace your steps back into the clearing and up to your car.

2.2 Arrive back at the trailhead.

7 The Old Briar Patch Trail

Take a stroll along these wooded trails where Thornton Burgess was inspired to write. Though the path begins steeply, the grade lessens along the first trail, making this trip suitable for most hikers. Keep your eyes peeled for wildlife and peeks of the Smiling Pool Pond.

Distance: 2.1-mile loop

Approximate hiking time: 1 hour

Difficulty: Easy/moderate

Trail surface: Hard packed soil

Best season: Year-round

Other trail users: None

Canine compatibility: Dog friendly

Fees and permits: None

Schedule: Dawn to dusk

Map: USGS Sandwich

Starting point: 6 Discovery Hill Road, East Sandwich

Trail contact: Green Briar Nature Center; www.thorntonburgess.org

Special considerations: Some narrow trails/steep hills

Finding the trailhead: To reach The Green Briar Nature Center from US 6, exit 3, travel north on Quaker Meeting House Road for 1 mile to MA 6A. Turn left (west) for 0.6 mile to Discovery Hill Road. Turn left (south) 0.2 mile to the center's parking area. GPS N41 44.758'/W070 28.204'

The Hike

Born in Sandwich on January 4, 1874, author Thornton W. Burgess, creator of the fictional characters of The Old Briar Patch, spent his youth exploring the wilds of Gully Lane. Writing whimsical animal stories for his small son led Burgess to become the noted author of 170 children's books and 15,000 bedtime stories. The Briar Patch Conservation

Area was dedicated by the Town of Sandwich in 1974 to permanently preserve the rolling hills and swampy lowland home of the many animals that inspired Burgess.

Named for the bull briars that form dense thickets wherever old pastures revert to woodlands, the Old Briar Patch is intertwined with marked trails that wander through a diversity of plant life. The Green Briar Nature Center, with its award-winning wildflower garden, herb garden, and frontage on the "Smiling Pool" pond, provides a delightful and interesting beginning.

The best way to enjoy this trail is to bring a Burgess story with you. Stop and read, then watch and listen for Peter and Mrs. Rabbit, Sammy Jay, Reddy Fox, Old Mr. Toad, Jimmy Skunk, or Bobby Coon.

Miles and Directions

0.0 The trail begins in the southwest corner of the parking area and is marked Briar Patch Trail. Follow it across the water district road and along the ledge behind the water district building to the first major intersection, marked Steep Hill Trail. Turn right.

0.4 Climb the Steep Hill Trail. At the top of the hill turn left (southeast), back into the woods. (For a shorter loop around the pond, stay to the left at each trail intersection.) Take the right (west) fork when the trail splits. Pass across the water pipe into the woods.

0.9 The trail meets the Gully Lane Trail. Turn left (southeast) on Gully Lane Trail, which veers to the right, reaching a three-way fork in the midst of a grove of black locust trees.

1.1 Arc sharply right down the Discovery Loop Trail. Climb Discovery Hill into a grove of white pines. Catch glimpses of the swamp below as you descend Discovery Hill.

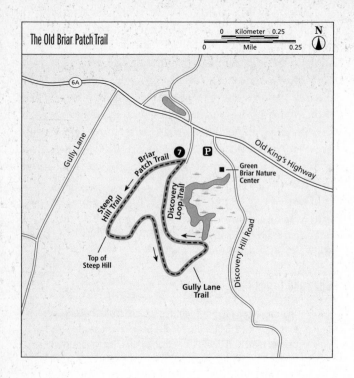

The Old Briar Patch Trail

0   Kilometer   0.25
0   Mile   0.25

N

6A

Gully Lane

Briar Patch Trail ⑦

Old King's Highway

Ⓟ

Green Briar Nature Center

Steep Hill Trail

Discovery Loop Trail

Top of Steep Hill

Gully Lane Trail

Discovery Hill Road

1.4 At the base of the hill, turn left (west) onto the Briar Patch Trail. This trail follows the wetland on the right. You will pass by the remains of an old boardwalk and through tupelos and beech. Shortly after you pass the Discovery Hill Loop Trail and a bench on the left, the Briar Patch Trail takes a sharp right.

1.8 The trail turns left up the steep hill just behind the water district building. Continue past the intersection with Steep Hill Trail, retracing your steps back to Green Briar Nature Center.

2.1 Arrive back at the trailhead.

8 Sandy Neck Barrier Beach

This barrier beach and the surrounding 3,000-acre Great Marsh is the most extensive conservation area outside of the Cape Cod National Seashore and the largest salt marsh complex on the Cape. The Great Marsh supports an abundance of marine life and provides protection and food for both sea and land birds.

Distance: 5.25-mile loop
Approximate hiking time: 2.5 hours
Difficulty: More challenging due to soft sand
Trail surface: Soft sand
Best season: Year-round
Other trail users: Hunters/off-road vehicles
Canine compatibility: Dog friendly (except 5/15–9/15); leashes enforced

Fees and permits: Day parking fee
Schedule: Dawn to dusk
Map: USGS Sandwich
Starting point: Sandy Neck Road, East Sandwich
Trail contact: Town of Barnstable; www.town.barnstable.ma.us/sandyneck
Special considerations: Seasonal restrooms

Finding the trailhead: To reach the Sandy Neck Nature Trail from US 6, Exit 3, travel north on Quaker Meeting House Road for 1 mile to MA 6A. Turn right (east) and go 3.1 miles to Sandy Neck Road. Turn left for 0.9 mile to the Ranger Station Guard House. Pay the fee and continue for another 0.3 mile to the paved parking area. GPS N41 44.0630'/W70 23.0731'

The Hike

Watch for great blue herons, willets, egrets, and other wading birds. Red-tailed hawks, kestrels, harriers, and other

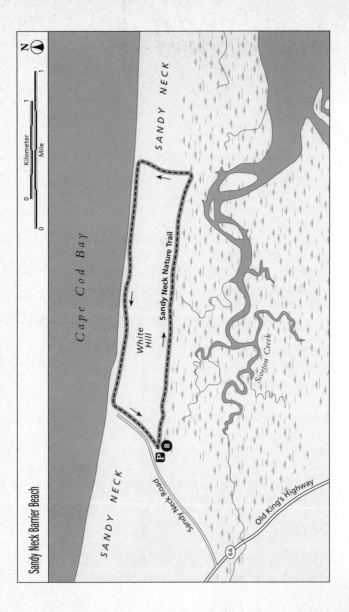

raptors may rise from the tall grasses. On the outer dunes and beach, look for the endangered piping plover or diamondback terrapin.

Large bare areas called "blowouts" often are caused by human abuse. Wild cherry, red cedar, greenbrier, Virginia creeper, and honeysuckle blend with the more common pitch pine, bearberry, beach plum, and bayberry in the thickets. Small "fish houses" come into view. Families owned these cottages long before the land was set aside as a reserve.

Unfortunately for human visitors, many insects also thrive in this environment. In an ill-conceived effort to control the bug population, long straight ditches were cut through the marsh to drain standing water. Today, raised wooden boxes trap the greenhead horsefly. Swallows, which feed on the flies, are attracted to nesting boxes along the trail. The insects still can be annoying here, so remember to wear insect repellent.

Soft sand makes this a more challenging hike. The sun can become unbearably hot and there is little shelter. Start early in the day and carry plenty of water. Prepare to be awed by the dunes, which peak high above you, as well as by the primitive, stubborn plant life and the isolated vastness of the marsh.

Miles and Directions

0.0 Begin by walking back (south), down the road for 0.3 mile from the parking area to the guard house. The area is open to hunting for periods during the fall and winter—check with a ranger before hiking. Directly across from the off-road vehicle entrance is a small wild cranberry bog. The trail begins opposite the guard house on the east side.

0.3 Reach the Sandy Neck Nature Trail and begin your walk in the soft sand east along the Great Marsh.

0.9 Pass the Trail 1 intersection where a mound of wild roses forms an island. Stay right (east), following the contours of the marsh. The small island on your right is private.

1.5 Take the left fork and do not trespass. You have been skirting the secondary or back dunes.

2.4 At the Trail 2 intersection, turn left toward the beach. Just past the secondary dunes, you enter the interdune swale. Less windy, the temperatures are warmer and the ground more arid. **Option:** Hike farther out on "the neck" into more remote areas. Inquire at the ranger station for more information.

2.7 Once you pass through the primary dunes, you can begin your walk back on the beach. Turn left, walking near the waterline to cool down. Stop for a rest or to picnic and take your time returning to climb the steps to the comfort station and parking area.

5.25 Arrive back at the trailhead.

The Middle Cape

If Cape Cod had a hub, the Middle Cape would be it. With its train station, ferry terminal, and airport, many travelers begin their visits here. Long and narrow, the Mid Cape includes the towns of Barnstable, Yarmouth, Dennis, Brewster, Harwich, Chatham, and Orleans.

The Mid Cape is generally flat and riddled with kettle ponds. Formed when dense glacial ice chunks melted among debris, these ponds vary in size and each one has its own personality. The relentless waves and wind that the terrain must absorb accounts for the Mid Cape's unique stunted vegetation of pitch pine, beech, and scrub oak. Tidal marshlands reach golden fingers to the sea and teem with migrating birds.

The north side retains its original early-American look, with tidy cottages tucked in the woods facing the sea, while the south side is known for warmer water and sunny beaches. Venturing beyond the famous shops and restaurants of the Mid Cape, its quieter spots will inspire you to return again and again.

$\mathcal{9}$ Callery-Darling Conservation Trails

Several trails wind through woodlands and across salt marshes in this narrow strip of conservation land. Beautiful and serene, the showstopper here is Gray's Beach with its spectacular dunes and half-mile boardwalk. Although not much of a beach, this is a playground for all who love shallow warm water.

Distance: 2.2 miles out and back

Approximate hiking time: 1 hour

Difficulty: Moderate

Trail surface: Asphalt, hard packed soil

Best season: Spring through fall

Other trail users: None

Canine compatibility: No dogs allowed

Fees and permits: Free parking

in lot; day parking fee 0.3 mile farther on Center Street

Schedule: Dawn to dusk

Map: USGS Dennis

Starting point: Alms House Road, Yarmouth

Trail contact: Yarmouth Department of Natural Resources; www .yarmouth.ma.us

Special considerations: Small lot closed in winter

Finding the trailhead: To reach the Callery-Darling Conservation Trails from US 6, exit 8, go north on Union Street for 1.2 miles to MA 6A. Zigzag across MA 6A north onto Old Church Road, which you will follow for 0.3 mile, until the road ends at Center Street. Turn right and follow Center for 0.7 mile to Alms House Road. Turn left; the small parking lot is an immediate right. GPS N41 43.158'/W070 14.053'

The Hike

This hike is an important part of the Mid Cape conservation area. You will encounter a variety of different habitats such as forest, thicket, and salt marsh.

Crabs, shrimp, and starfish can be found in the sand between marsh and beach grass. The tide whispers into this incredible bay, lapping the grasses into motion. Mesmerizing and delightful, it is difficult to leave.

This trail is flat and easy, with diversity around every corner. Check the tides before you go. High tide makes many spots soupy. Bring binoculars and a magnifying glass so you can catch all the sights, from magnificent shore birds and herons to tiny marsh creatures.

Miles and Directions

0.0   The trail begins in the northeast corner of the parking area. A map of the trails is posted just beyond the trailhead. Take the left fork, north through lowlands. Turn left onto Center Street and walk past the parking lot to the water and the boardwalk.

0.4   Stroll out onto the boardwalk all the way to the benches at its end. Enjoy the sea breeze and the incredible view before you return to the parking lot (0.6 mile round-trip). Cut across the parking area to the grassy hill. Circle the picnic pavilion, walk past the small playground (unless you are with little ones), and head to the trailhead (look very closely for a wood post marking the trail) in the southeast corner of the clearing.

1.3   The trail leads out into the saltwater marsh. Boards have been placed to help you keep your feet dry. Jump the small drainage ditch, circle to your left through 10-foot-high phragmites reeds, and climb up to higher ground.

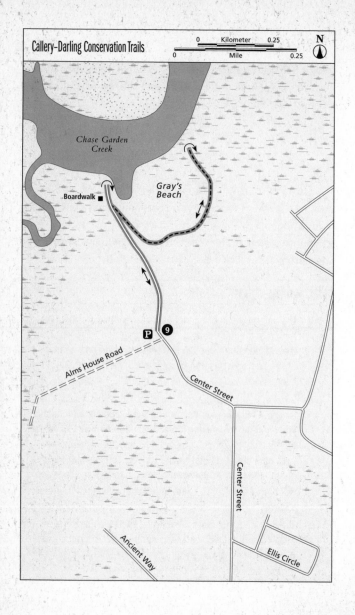

Callery-Darling Conservation Trails

Kilometer
0   0.25
0   0.25
Mile

N

Chase Garden Creek

Boardwalk ■

Gray's Beach

P **9**

Alms House Road

Center Street

Center Street

Ancient Way

Ellis Circle

1.7 Turn right at the first trail fork, then right again at the next trail intersection, heading west. The woodlands of pine and oak sparkle with holly, and pine needles cushion the trail. Continue down the steps to cross Center Street and return to the parking area.

2.2 Arrive back at the trailhead.

10 Indian Lands Conservation Area Trail

Don't be fooled by the start of this trail under the power lines. Once you pass the trailhead, this loop explores a small nook of the Bass River and allows you to observe blue herons, search for tree swallows, or watch marsh hawks.

Distance: 1.7-mile lollipop
Approximate hiking time: 45 minutes
Difficulty: Easy
Trail surface: Hard packed soil
Best season: All seasons
Other trail users: None
Canine compatibility: Dog friendly
Fees and permits: None

Schedule: Dawn to dusk
Map: USGS Dennis
Starting point: 485 Main Street, South Dennis
Trail contact: Dennis Conservation Department; www.town. dennis.ma.us/dept/naturalres/ natresources.htm
Special considerations: None

Finding the trailhead: To reach the Indian Lands Trail from US 6, exit 9A, go south 0.9 mile on MA 134 to the third traffic light. Turn right (west) onto Upper County Road. Take the right (north) fork to Main Street and turn right. After 0.2 mile, park in the north side of the Dennis Town Offices parking lot. GPS N41 41.417'/W070 09.444'

The Hike

The banks of the Bass River were once home to the Pawkannawkut Indians, a tribe that was part of the Wampanoag Nation, which held sovereignty over the vast area from Cape Cod north to Massachusetts Bay. The Pawkannawkut camped and hunted along the river shores until a smallpox epidemic wiped out the tribe in the 1770s. They called their home Mattacheset, meaning "old or planting lands by the borders of the water." They planted beans, pumpkins, and corn in natural and manmade clearings.

Later, settlers harvested soft salt marsh hay. They cut and piled it on horse-drawn wagons and took it to the uplands where they laid it out to dry. They used the hay for cattle feed and mulch and spread it around the foundations of their drafty homes for insulation.

Today, the Bass River marsh is an important wetland habitat. Cattails provide tender roots for muskrats to eat and perches for red-winged blackbirds. Needles cushion your steps in the pitch pines, and it becomes easy to imagine a dugout canoe gliding softly on the expanse of the river as you relax at an overlook.

Miles and Directions

0.0 The trailhead is well marked with a conservation sign. A wide sandy path runs alongside railroad tracks and under power line poles. The wooded trail begins just over the rise.

0.4 As the wooded trail begins, turn left (south) onto the trail. A map is posted before you enter the woodlands. Stay left (west) at the Y intersection. A brackish pond is on your left and you can catch glimpses of the marsh to your right. The Bass River comes into view, and you will walk across a narrow strip of land separating it from the marsh.

0.7 Stay left (southwest) at the fork, following the shoreline of the Bass River. In the distance you can see cars traveling across a bridge, and as you make a sweeping right turn, beautiful homes with private docks come into view. A bench perches on a lovely overlook at this point and a quaint picnic table follows around the corner. Continue north on the

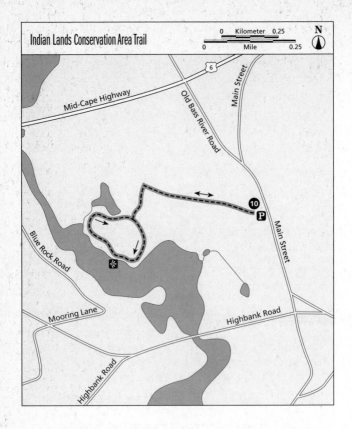

path to the marsh. Walk quietly around the sharp right (east) turn, as the birds are easily startled. Scan the expanse of marsh for ducks of all varieties and three different types of heron. Before you know it, you will have completed the loop.

1.3 Turn left (north), crossing back over the dike and past the brackish pond to the first trail intersection. Stay right (north) to the power lines. Turn right again to return to the parking area.

1.7 Arrive back at the trailhead.

11 Cape Cod Museum of Natural History Trails

Escape the crowds and enjoy one of the most beautiful spots on the Cape. This scenic hike lands you on an expansive beach with endless tidepools at low tide and breathtaking vistas in every direction.

Distance: Two lollipops consisting of John Wing Trail at 1.3 miles and South Trail at 1.5 miles

Approximate hiking time: 1 hour

Difficulty: Easy/moderate

Trail surface: Packed soil, sections of soft sand

Best season: All seasons

Other trail users: Students of museum

Canine compatibility: Dog friendly

Fees and permits: None

Schedule: Dawn to dusk

Map: USGS Harwich

Starting point: 869 Main Street, Brewster

Trail contact: Cape Cod Museum of Natural History; www.ccmnh.org

Special considerations: Parking is used for museum also

Finding the trailhead: To reach the Cape Cod Museum of Natural History from US 6, exit 9B, go north on MA 134 for 3.9 miles to MA 6A. Turn right (east) for 2.5 miles to the well-marked entrance to the Cape Cod Museum of Natural History parking lot. GPS N41 45.228'/ W070 07.004'

The Hikes

Three excellent trails, all within the Stony Brook watershed, offer a wonderful introduction to the diversity of the Cape landscape. Walk through upland woods, across salt marshes, near fresh and saltwater creeks, or stretch your toes in a sandy beach. Offering something for everyone, from a short, easy loop to challenging hills, these hikes are Cape musts. Two of the trails—the John Wing Trail and the South Trail—are described here.

The North Trail is a short, 0.25-mile loop perfect for the very young. Numbered stations identify native flora. Wildflowers flourish and the views of the salt marsh and Paine's Creek are breathtaking.

The John Wing Trail explores Wing Island, once the site of a farm and salt works. Inhabited by 1653, the island was first used to harvest salt hay. The trail crosses the marsh, winds through the uplands, and then descends to a barrier beach and Cape Cod Bay.

The South Trail passes through a salt marsh and over Paine's Creek, a major migration route for alewives, or Cape Cod herring. Pilgrims used alewives as food and to fertilize corn fields. Circle through a unique beech forest to the eastern bank of Stony Brook. Walk gingerly through the forest as the roots from these beautiful trees mingle in the cut paths.

Miles and Directions

John Wing Trail

0.0 The trail begins on the northwest side of the museum buildings. A boardwalk crosses the marsh (high tide may flood the walkway—check with museum staff). A sign welcomes you to Wing Island.

0.2 Turn right at marker 4. A monument to John Wing is on the right. Pass through a clearing of tall cedars and then through a hedge.

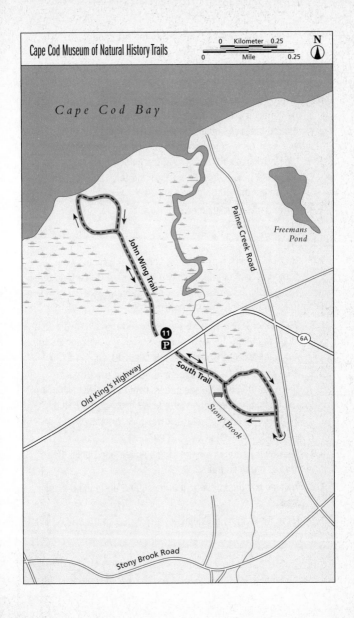

Cape Cod Museum of Natural History Trails

Cape Cod Bay

Freemans Pond

Paines Creek Road

John Wing Trail

6A

11
P

Old King's Highway

South Trail

Stony Brook

Stony Brook Road

N

0   Kilometer   0.25

0   Mile   0.25

0.5 Make a sharp left at the trail fork and hike north along a ridge. At the top of the rise, turn left (the right fork is a short path to an overlook of Brewster Flats). The trail winds into a pitch pine forest.

0.7 Turn right at the trail intersection, then continue straight past marker 7 to an overlook. For a longer walk, climb down around massive boulders and cross the marsh on one of the well-worn trails to reach the beach. Or you can walk back past marker 7 and turn right at the first trail crossing, then left at the next intersection. Follow the trail straight ahead, across the marsh to the parking area.

1.3 Arrive back at the trailhead.

South Trail

0.0 This trail begins across MA 6A from the museum on the southeast side of the overflow parking area. Descend to the salt marsh and cross Paine's Creek, then make a sharp left and climb up into the beech forest.

0.3 Walk along a ledge above the creek and through a gully to a sharp right turn. The path becomes needle-cushioned as you reach the top of the Beech Forest Loop.

0.5 Stay left at the Y intersection and descend toward Stony Brook; at the next intersection, go right to a lovely overlook. The trail arcs sharply right into dense thickets. Wind through the lowlands; the thickets give way to lush ferns as you approach the bank of Stony Brook.

0.9 After pausing to admire the brook, go left and uphill, then drop to the main trail.

1.2 Walk across the bridge in the marsh and up to the parking area.

1.5 Arrive back at the trailhead.

12 Harding's Beach

This is the perfect sunset beach stroll. Harding's Beach is a spit of sand dividing the ocean from Oyster River and Stage Harbor. Plan to watch the sun set into Nantucket Sound or bring a picnic and stay the day.

Distance: 2.0-mile loop
Approximate hiking time: 45 minutes
Difficulty: Moderate/more challenging
Trail surface: Soft sand
Best season: All seasons
Other trail users: Lighthouse caretakers' access drive
Canine compatibility: No dogs allowed 4/1–9/15

Fees and permits: Parking fee in summer
Schedule: Dawn to dusk
Map: USGS Chatham
Starting point: Harding's Beach Road, Chatham
Trail contact: Chatham Planning Board; www.mychatham.com/hardingsbeach
Special considerations: Soft sand

Finding the trailhead: To reach Harding's Beach from US 6, exit 11, go south on MA 137 for 3.2 miles, going straight through the four-way intersection with blinking lights. MA 137 ends at MA 28; turn left (east) and drive for 1.5 miles. Turn right (south) at the blinking light onto Barn Hill Road. Go 0.4 mile and bear right at the fork onto Harding's Beach Road. Follow this 0.9 mile to the beach entrance (a seasonal parking fee is charged). Drive through the first lot into the smaller lot. The trail begins as a soft sand road at the south end of the lot. GPS N41 40.022'/W069 59.714'

The Hike

A tribute to Chatham's history with the sea, Harding's Light has stood sentry at the entrance to Stage Harbor for

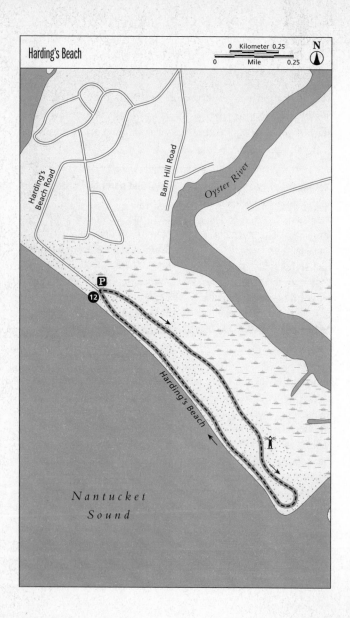

hundreds of years. Privately owned, it was marred by a storm that toppled the top of the light itself.

In Oyster River, a saltwater inlet, fishermen grow and harvest oysters and naturally flourishing bay scallops. Common terns dive for their next meal, and if you're lucky, you may see a pair of horned larks. This lark is attracted by the sparsely vegetated land and moves by walking rather than hopping across the sand.

The views are spectacular. Across Nantucket Sound is low, sandy Monomoy Island. Directly across the harbor entrance is Morris Island, which is actually a peninsula extending south from Chatham.

Roll up your pant legs, sink your toes into the sand, and relish the cool surf. Search for perfect shells in the seaweed mounds left by the last high tide, or watch fiddler crabs dance close to the water. Take some time to savor the beauty of this stretch of white sand before returning to your car.

Miles and Directions

0.0 To begin, trek through the soft sand on the road past salt spray roses and beach plum. Enjoy the views of Oyster River to your left.

0.5 Stay to the right when the road forks, staying southeast and out of the marsh. Sand is replaced by gravel, which makes the walking easier. Stage Harbor opens in front and to the left of you, with its small fishing boats secure at their moorings.

0.8 Follow the soft sand to the right of the private driveway for Harding's Light. Pass in front of the lighthouse, through the dunes and onto the beach. Turn back and head north past a small tidal pool on the beach.

2.0 Arrive back at the trailhead.

13 Morris Island Trail

On the tip of Morris Island, this trail shadows Nantucket Sound. Very steep stairs and soft sand may make this a less attractive hike for the faint of heart. If you attempt the hike, you will be rewarded with breathtaking views and an occasional seal sighting. This is a must-see for the ocean lover.

Distance: 1.4-mile lollipop
Approximate hiking time: 40 minutes
Difficulty: Moderate/more challenging
Trail surface: Steep stairs, soft sand
Best season: All seasons
Other trail users: None
Canine compatibility: Dog friendly—leashes enforced
Fees and permits: None

Schedule: Dawn to dusk; trail is closed for one hour before and one hour after high tide
Map: USGS Chatham
Starting point: Morris Island Road, Chatham
Trail contact: Monomoy National Wildlife Refuge; www.fws.gov/northeast/monomoy
Special considerations: Soft sand; long, steep stairs down to beach; seasonal restrooms

Finding the trailhead: To reach the Morris Island Trail from MA 28 at the Chatham Rotary, go straight (east) onto Main Street and follow it 0.9 mile to its end. Turn right on the unmarked extension of Main Street. Go 0.5 mile, past Chatham Light and the parking area. Curve to the right, then take the first left onto Morris Island Road. Drive 1 mile to Tisquantum Road and turn left (follow the Monomoy National Wildlife Refuge signs). You will see signs for a private neighborhood. Keep driving as you immediately turn left on Wikis Way into the parking lot after entering the neighborhood. GPS N41 39.5034'/W69 57.6251'

The Hike

Morris Island offers a small sampling of the unique habitats of the Monomoy Islands and is the only section of Monomoy National Wildlife Refuge accessible by land. Countless shore birds, waterfowl, and songbirds rest, feed, and nurture their young here. During certain times of the year, seals frolic offshore in the shallow waters.

Monomoy once was a peninsula, then an island, and is now two islands. The constant shifting of sand and sea is evident in the refuge and provides a wonderful introduction to the Cape's seashore and its inhabitants. Gentle waves wash the white sand beach, making it a perfect playground for little ones.

Note: The trail is closed for one hour before and one hour after high tide. Check tide charts before you leave.

Miles and Directions

0.0 Begin by following the trail to the cliff overlooking North and South Monomoy Islands and get an overview of your excursion. Return to the main trail, which descends steep steps and navigates through a tangle of downed trees to the beach.

0.4 After chasing the surf and inspecting the shore for treasures, a sign directs you to the trail, which is cut through the dunes to the right. Stop to read the informational signs, which start in the stabilized dunes, before heading into an area of woody plants behind the dunes, which are protected from the open waters.

0.6 The Salt Marsh Pond, with its tall grasses and reeds, is habitat for numerous shorebirds and some ocean fish. Follow the

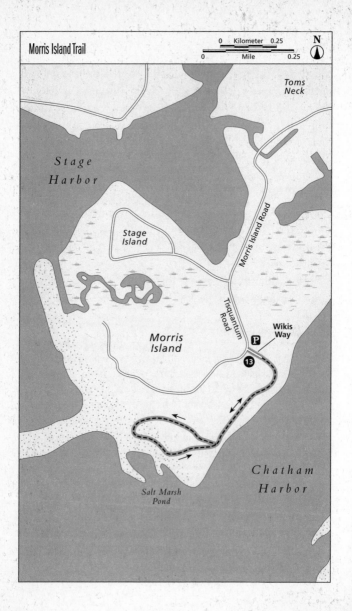

Morris Island Trail

| 0 | Kilometer | 0.25 |
| 0 | Mile | 0.25 |

N

Stage
Harbor

Toms
Neck

Morris Island Road

Stage
Island

Tisquantum Road

Morris
Island

P

Wikis
Way

13

Chatham
Harbor

Salt Marsh
Pond

trail as it rims the marsh. Complete the loop on the beach. If you choose, linger on the beach to rest in the sun or do some beachcombing before heading back up the steps to the parking area.

1.4 Arrive back at the trailhead.

14 Cliff Pond Trail

This hike follows the contours of the pond and is made slightly more challenging with climbs in and out of the woods. While sauntering under a canopy of trees, enjoy the cooling breezes and views of the glistening pond. If you so desire, bring your fishing pole and stop and sit at one of the outlets to the trail and try your luck.

Distance: 3.9-mile loop
Approximate hiking time: 1.5 hours
Difficulty: Easy/moderate
Trail surface: Hard packed soil
Best season: All seasons
Other trail users: Anglers
Canine compatibility: Dog friendly
Fees and permits: None for day parking—only if camping
Schedule: Dawn to dusk
Map: USGS Harwich
Starting point: 3488 Main Street, Brewster
Trail contact: Nickerson State Park; www.mass.gov/dcr/parks/southeast.nick.htm
Special considerations: Some sections of trail narrow and steep

Finding the trailhead: To reach the Cliff Pond Trail at Nickerson State Park from US 6, exit 12, go west on Main Street, away from Orleans. The entrance to the park is 1.6 miles beyond the exit, and is clearly marked. Turn left (south) and drive through the gate. Go 0.2 mile to the sign marked AREA 5. Turn left and travel 0.5 mile past the Area 5 turnoff and Flax Pond Beach. The road ends in a parking area above the East Fisherman's Landing boat ramp. GPS N41 45.633'/ W070 01.110'

The Hike

Cliff Pond is one of the largest kettle ponds on the Cape. Beautiful, clear water is surrounded by crescent-shaped beaches rimmed with pines and oaks.

The pond is stocked twice each year, attracting fishermen who wait patiently in their waders along the shore or quietly in small boats or canoes. A still bay on the southern shore and two small pools at either end encourage waterfowl to congregate.

Long pants will protect your legs from the short brush that threatens to clog some parts of the trail. Many small beaches offer great spots to picnic or relax.

Miles and Directions

0.0 The Cliff Pond trailhead is well marked on the northwest side of the parking area. The trail climbs through low brush. A clearing at the top of the hill shelters picnic tables.

0.2 The trail makes a short right jog and descends a steep bank to the water's edge. The path turns sandy and passes small beaches before heading up into the woods.

0.9 The path descends to the shore again, where two giant boulders stand sentry on the north side of the pond. Cross a ravine created by rain water. A sandy dike separates the pond from a small pool on your right.

1.9 You will reach the West Fisherman's Landing parking area. Walk straight across the lot to the southwest corner and follow the trail up into the woods. Turn left (east) at the T intersection onto a wider trail, and left again at the Y intersection following the blue blazes. Cross yet another trail intersection and ascend a small bluff to the right above the pond. Turn left at the next two intersections.

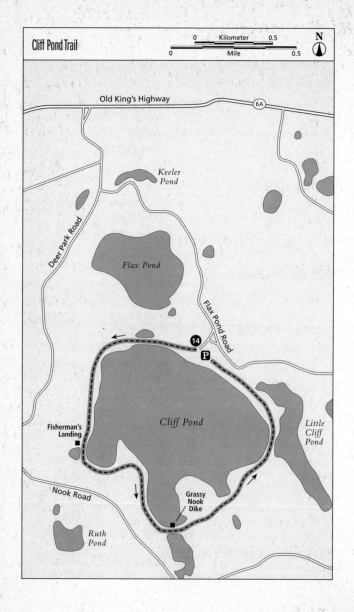

Cliff Pond Trail

| 0 | Kilometer | 0.5 |
| 0 | Mile | 0.5 |

N

Old King's Highway

6A

Keeler Pond

Deer Park Road

Flax Pond

Flax Pond Road

14

P

Fisherman's Landing

Cliff Pond

Little Cliff Pond

Nook Road

Grassy Nook Dike

Ruth Pond

2.8 A sandy dike separates Cliff Pond from Grassy Nook Pond. Bear left, staying close to the Cliff Pond shore; the path becomes rocky.

3.2 A large sandy beach makes a wonderful resting spot. Pick up the trail close to the shoreline and follow it over a small rise to the last dike, which separates Cliff Pond from Little Cliff Pond. You will walk through a wooded area before crossing a small beach; the parking area is just beyond.

3.9 Arrive back at the trailhead.

The Lower Cape

The Lower Cape, or "Outer Cape," is the sandy finger beckoning sailors and travelers to Massachusetts. The tip of Cape Cod, surf-washed and so narrow that at certain points both coasts are visible, has attracted artists for centuries with its unique landscape.

The Cape Cod National Seashore, 27,000 acres of bluffs and sand, occupies more than half of the Lower Cape's land mass and defines the character of this part of Cape Cod. Preserved by John F. Kennedy in 1961, the landscape in this national park constantly changes. Reforestation has begun in many areas, sand dunes are reshaped in every storm, and the tide provides a twice-daily washing of the extensive wetlands.

Whether you are exploring nature's reclaiming of land once tamed by man, becoming awestruck at the vastness of the dunes, or savoring the lingering sun on a deserted beach, the magic of the sand and sea will sweep you up in its beauty.

15 Fort Hill Trail

In addition to tremendous vistas, this trail offers a good workout and spectacular birding. The boardwalk is expansive and unique to trails on the cape, and much needed in this very swampy hike. Mosquitoes thrive in this environment, so be sure to bring your bug spray if you visit in the summertime.

Distance: 1.8 miles out and back
Approximate hiking time: 30 minutes
Difficulty: Easy
Trail surface: Hard packed soil, decking, asphalt
Best season: All seasons
Other trail users: None
Canine compatibility: No dogs allowed
Fees and permits: None
Schedule: 7 a.m.–9 p.m.
Map: USGS Orleans
Starting point: Fort Hill Road, Orleans
Trail contact: Cape Cod National Seashore; www.nps.gov/caco
Special considerations: None

Finding the trailhead: To reach the Fort Hill Trail, drive 1.5 miles north on US 6 from the Orleans Rotary. At the signs for the Fort Hill area, turn right onto Governor Prence Road. At the Y intersection, turn left onto Fort Hill Road. Pass the Penniman House on the right and park in the small lot just past it on the left (0.3 mile total from US 6). GPS N41 49.127'/W069 57.874'

The Hike

Great blue herons sweep over the marsh and the notes of songbirds fill the air. Wander through the Red Maple Swamp, where boardwalks curl through cinnamon and wood ferns under aged red maples.

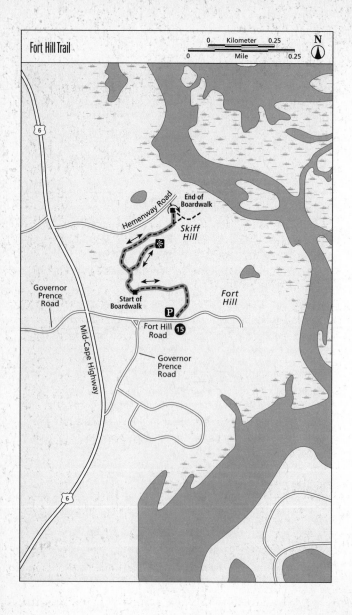

Edge Nauset Marsh, ascend Skiff Hill, and continue over Indian Rock. Found at the base of the cliff, without the benefit of surrounding artifacts, its unique scratched surface remains a mystery.

During the season, take the time to visit the Penniman House. Highlighted with a whalebone archway, this Victorian home was once the most elegant in Eastham.

Miles and Directions

0.0 The trail begins at the northeast corner of the parking lot. Climb a few log steps up to a meadow. At the first trail intersection, turn left, following the sign marked RED MAPLE SWAMP. Descend into the swamp down a set of steps. A boardwalk meanders through and around the shallow water.

0.3 Go left where the trail splits. Another section of boardwalk leads to drier ground through hedges of fox grapes. The trail twists and turns, eventually making a sharp right, heading east. Planks rebuilt with recycled material keep your feet dry.

0.7 Reach a three-way trail and turn right and stroll out to the overlook for a rest and a breathtaking view. When you're ready, continue back on the boardwalk and straight up the steps to a paved path. Continue right on the paved path to Skiff Hill.

0.9 Enjoy the view and scan Nauset Marsh for birds. Head back down to the trailhead.

1.1 Pass the first trail crossing to Red Maple Swamp and retrace your steps downhill to the parking area.

1.8 Arrive back at the trailhead.

16 Salt Pond Visitor Center Trails

This spectacular loop edges Salt Pond as well as the bay. With marshy sections, the tide can be an issue, but the views once you cross into the wooded section are well worth the wait. Intermingled with private homes as well as the Cape Cod Rail Trail, this walk is definitely a gem.

Distance: 1.25-mile loop
Approximate hiking time: 35 minutes
Difficulty: Easy/moderate
Trail surface: Soft sand, hard packed soil, asphalt
Best season: All seasons
Other trail users: None
Canine compatibility: No dogs allowed
Fees and permits: None

Schedule: 6 a.m.–midnight; trail is sometimes closed during high tide
Map: USGS Eastham
Starting point: Nauset Road, Eastham
Trail contact: Cape Cod National Seashore; www.nps.gov/caco
Special considerations: Visitor center open 9 a.m.–4:30 p.m.; seasonal bathrooms

Finding the trailhead: To reach the Salt Pond Visitor Center, follow US 6 north from the Orleans Rotary for 3.1 miles. Turn right at the well-marked visitor center entrance on Nauset Road. The parking area is 0.1 mile on the right. GPS N41 50.254'/W069 58.286'

The Hikes

The Buttonbush Trail, 0.25 mile long, is designed for the visually impaired. This is a trail of contrasting surfaces, sudden temperature changes, and plenty of sounds. Equipped with Braille and large-print markers, this flat easy trail circles Buttonbush Pond, offering an interesting introduction to its inhabitants.

The Nauset Marsh Trail includes half of the Buttonbush Trail, so it isn't necessary to do both. Gradual ascents weave through gentle rolling countryside filled with cedars and bayberry; the path dips down to wind along the shoreline of Nauset Marsh and Salt Pond. Overlooks offer you the chance to reflect on expansive, water-filled views.

Each decade brings change to the Nauset Marsh. The buildup of the narrow barrier beach, Nauset Spit, allowed the marsh to flourish, and the ocean formed a narrow channel linking an original freshwater pond to the sea, creating Salt Pond. Today, the marsh and pond are home to abundant plant and animal life.

Check with the folks in the visitor center before beginning this hike. During high tide, especially in the spring, the trail may be closed.

The Buttonbush Trail begins on the upper left (east) side of the amphitheater at the south side of the parking lot. A guide rope leads from marker to marker as you wind around the pond. A boardwalk raises you above the pond's surface. The trail intersects with Nauset Marsh Trail and the bicycle trail.

Cross a small section of trail that does not have a guide rope to complete the loop. A slight rise takes you into a wooded area above the pond. Study the different trees and bushes, both native and introduced. End this trail where you began.

Miles and Directions

0.0 Start on the lower right side (southwest corner) of the amphitheater at the south side of the parking lot. You quickly reach Salt Pond's shoreline where you turn left. Walk the pond's edge, which, depending on the tide, may be dry

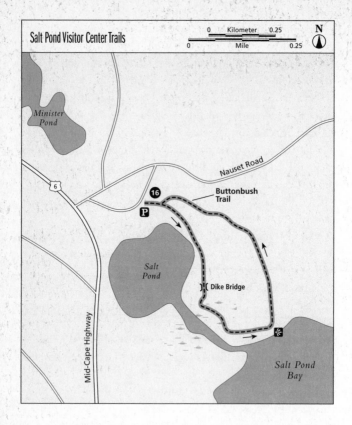

Minister Pond

Nauset Road

16

P

Buttonbush Trail

Salt Pond

Dike Bridge

Mid-Cape Highway

Salt Pond Bay

or spongy masses of salt hay. A boardwalk protects you from all but the highest tide on the far end of the pond.

0.2 Curve sharply to the left along the flow of sea water entering the pond. Make a gradual ascent, following the ledge around another left curve.

0.4 Cross the dike on a wooden bridge, then stay right at the trail fork and climb a series of log steps. Stay on the trail, respecting private property (trail marked with a sign with a hiker). Continue on the log-lined main trail up to a lookout.

0.6 Leaving the lookout, if you have the energy, turn right onto the Doane Memorial Trail (marked with a sign), which is at the bottom of the hill. It is 0.9 mile each way. Otherwise, continue straight through the wooded hills. Cross the bike path into an area that was once farmed. Black locust trees were planted here to replenish the soil.

1.0 Cross the bike path again two times and then go straight onto the Buttonbush Trail back to the parking area.

1.25 Arrive back at the trailhead.

17 Great Island Trail

This is the one of the most fascinating hikes on Cape Cod. The trail follows a saltwater marsh across a dike of sand that transformed Great Island into a peninsula.

Distance: 3.6 miles out and back
Approximate hiking time: 2.5 hours
Difficulty: More challenging due to soft sand
Trail surface: Soft sand
Best season: All seasons
Other trail users: None
Canine compatibility: No dogs allowed
Fees and permits: None
Schedule: Dawn to dusk
Map: USGS Wellfleet
Starting point: Kendrick Avenue, Wellfleet
Trail contact: Cape Cod National Seashore; www.nps.gov/caco
Special considerations: Check tides

Finding the trailhead: To reach the Great Island Trail, drive 11.6 miles north on US 6 from the Orleans Rotary to the light at the sign for Wellfleet Center. Turn left onto Main Street and go for 0.3 mile. Turn left, down the hill, onto Commercial Street for 0.7 mile. At the Town Pier, make a sharp right onto Kendrick Avenue. Travel on Kendrick Avenue 2.6 miles, staying left at the Y intersection, passing the public beach and going over the causeway. Just beyond the public recreation area lot, turn left at the sign for Great Island. GPS N41 55.966'/W070 04.145'

The Hike

Great Island is wild and windswept, with a small stunted pine forest, vast bearberry- and lichen-covered dunes, and miles of sandy beach that narrow to Jeremy Point, pointing a bony finger toward Brewster.

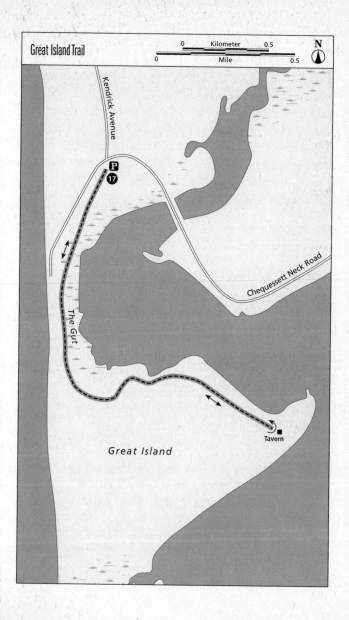

Great Island Trail

Kendrick Avenue

P 17

The Gut

Chequessett Neck Road

Great Island

Tavern

It was into this bay that the Pilgrims sailed on their second exploration. Later, whalers congregated on Great Island. This trail leads to the site of a whaler's tavern and is one of several hike options for exploring the island.

There is little shade, so start early to avoid midday summer sun. Low tide is the best time, as the trail disappears at times at high tide. Erosion is a major problem on the island: Stay on established trails and off the fragile dunes.

Options

Plow west through the dunes to Chequesset Beach for some sun, or walk as far south on the beach as you wish. To reach Jeremy Point, you must hike 4.1 miles one way from the parking area. Much of the point is submerged except at the lowest tide. Consult local tide charts.

Miles and Directions

0.0 The trail begins on the left side of the parking area as you enter. Descend on the gravel path to the edge of the marsh.

0.2 Turn right and circle the marsh on the mud flats. Stay on the inside of the fence, off the dunes.

0.7 As you make the left turn, you will be on the "gut," the tombolo that connects the peninsula to the mainland. Continue straight past the end of the fence and turn left again, following the edge of the marsh.

1.2 Before you reach the bay, a trail leads into the woods. Follow the trail markers to the yet-to-be-excavated tavern.

1.8 Reach the tavern, then return to the main trail at the marsh edge. Retrace your steps back to the gut. From the northwest corner of the marsh, turn right to return the way you came, around the marsh and up to the parking area.

3.6 Arrive back at the trailhead.

18 Pilgrim Spring Trail and Small's Swamp Trail

Pilgrim Spring and Small's Swamp are two trails that wind around and above a kettle swamp and marsh formed when a buildup of sand closed off the ocean in 1869. The trails together form a figure 8. An interpretive shelter provides information, and the trails are well marked with historical and nature signposts.

Distance: 1.3 miles consisting of two short loops (Pilgrim Spring at 0.5 mile and Small's Swamp at 0.8 mile)

Approximate hiking time: 35 minutes for both loops

Difficulty: Easy

Trail surface: Hard packed soil

Best season: All seasons

Other trail users: None

Canine compatibility: No dogs allowed

Fees and permits: None

Schedule: Dawn to dusk

Map: USGS North Truro

Starting point: Pilgrim Heights Road, Truro

Trail contact: Cape Cod National Seashore; www.nps.gov/caco

Special considerations: None

Finding the trailhead: To reach the Pilgrim Spring and Small's Swamp Trails, follow US 6 for 21.5 miles north from the Orleans Rotary. Turn right onto the road marked Pilgrim Heights. Follow the arrows for 0.5 mile to the parking area near the interpretive shelter. The trails begin at the far end of the parking area near the shelter. If you park in the lower lot, follow the short trail to the upper parking area, do the Small's Swamp Trail, and then Pilgrim Spring Trail, which ends in the lower lot. GPS N42 3.3247'/W070 6.4032'

The Hikes

The Pilgrim Spring and Small's Swamp Trails share a gazebo shelter at the trailhead equipped with picnic tables so you may enjoy a meal during your hike. Although both walks are short, these trails offer impressive views of East Harbor Creek, Pilgrim Lake, sand dunes, the salt meadow, and the Atlantic Ocean.

Pilgrim Spring Trail leads through a pitch pine forest to Pilgrim Spring. Although historians argue about its exact location and date, a stone marker identifies the probable site of the first fresh water the Pilgrims found. Overlooking a marsh and what's left of East Harbor Creek, the small spring bubbles up near a bramble patch.

Small's Swamp Trail explores the remains of Thomas Small's farm and circles the kettle swamp. Nothing remains of Small's efforts except his grape, lilac, plum, and apple plantings. Untamed now, they blend with the swamp azaleas, highbush blueberries, bearberry, and the returning woods.

Miles and Directions

Pilgrim Spring Trail:

0.0 Begin by heading northeast, down into the pitch pine forest of odd, windswept trees. Pine needles make interesting patterns on the sandy trail. Climb up a short rise to an overlook for a breathtaking view. Then, follow the trail down to the spring.

0.2 At the PILGRIM SPRING marker, start the ascent to the parking area southwest of the spring. (The paved trail below is the Head of the Meadow Bicycle Trail.) Climb switchbacks up to the lower parking area. Cross the parking lot, go up the sandy path to the upper lot, and head back to the shelter.

0.5 Arrive back at the trailhead.

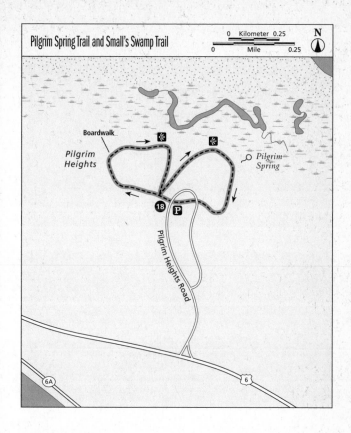

Boardwalk

*Pilgrim
Heights*

18

P

Pilgrim Heights Road

*Pilgrim &
Spring*

6A

6

Small's Swamp Trail:

0.0 This trail starts by descending to a pitch pine grove. Turn left at the trail fork and follow the rough-hewn fence down the steps and back and forth on the switchbacks into the kettle swamp.

0.3 The sandy path goes through a berry patch and circles the swampy lowlands. One long boardwalk keeps you dry across the wettest spot. Enjoy the cool beech forest and then climb the steps cut out of bearberry.

0.6 Three markers identify features of the outstanding view below as you traverse the edge of the bluff. Head back into the forest. Turn left at the fork and retrace your steps to the parking lot.

0.8 Arrive back at the trailhead.

19 Beech Forest Trail

The Beech Forest Trail follows the edges of a freshwater pond, then rambles through a beech forest mixed with native pitch pine and scrub oak. A quick walk, this is a great way to familiarize yourself with the Cape landscape. On your way out, be sure to continue past the trailhead on Race Point Road to the visitor center. The views are well worth the trip.

Distance: 1.0-mile loop
Approximate hiking time: 25 minutes
Difficulty: Easy
Trail surface: Hard packed soil
Best season: All seasons
Other trail users: None
Canine compatibility: No dogs allowed

Fees and permits: None
Schedule: Dawn to dusk
Map: USGS Provincetown
Starting point: Race Point Road, Provincetown
Trail contact: Cape Cod National Seashore; www.nps.gov/caco
Special considerations: None

Finding the trailhead: To reach the Beech Forest Trail, follow US 6 north for 26.4 miles from the Orleans Rotary. Turn right at the traffic light onto Race Point Road. The Beech Forest Trail parking area is 0.5 mile beyond on the left. GPS N42 04.004'/W070 11.626'

The Hike

Thriving forests once blanketed the northernmost tip of Cape Cod, but early settlers showed little concern for natural resources. Clear-cutting, overgrazing, and forest fires obliterated the native landscape. By the 1800s, shifting dunes threatened to destroy the Province Lands settlements.

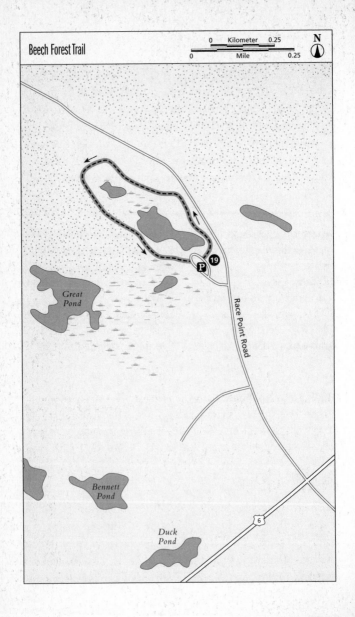

0   Kilometer   0.25

0   Mile   0.25

N

P 19

Great Pond

Race Point Road

Bennett Pond

Duck Pond

6

Strict conservation controls began and beach grass was planted, stabilizing the dunes' movements.

Now, parts of this vast land have been reforested and fresh water has collected in low spots. Visit the small pond on the return portion of the loop by using short spur trails. Approach quietly to be greeted with the bulging eyes and croaking voices of frogs. Many species of ducks and wading birds call the ponds home, and you might catch a glimpse of a turtle.

The salt spray rose, or *rosa rugosa*, thrives in the sandy soil: Look for the delicate magenta or white blossoms. In the spring, thick yellow lilies cover the pond's surface.

Miles and Directions

0.0 The trail begins at the northeast corner of the parking lot. Log-lined, it enters the pitch pine forest and traverses on boardwalks over low spots. Soft sand slows your progress through a small clearing.

0.3 At the first trail intersection go straight into the beech forest. The pathway is paved for a short distance as it winds its way up into the woods.

0.7 Steps bring you down to the pond. Skirt the opposite bank of the pond and then walk between it and a smaller pond. A small plank wharf provides a resting spot overlooking the smaller pond. The trail ends at the opposite side of the parking area.

1.0 Arrive back at the trailhead.

The Islands

South of Cape Cod lie two islands that are different in almost every way: landscape, history, and temperament. Martha's Vineyard, the larger and closer of the two, has an agricultural base. Forest dominates its interior and unspoiled beaches ring the coasts. The island of Nantucket once was the greatest whaling center in the world; economic decline has preserved Nantucket Town and its cobblestone streets.

The two islands share the same glacial roots, although the Nauset Tribe explains their beginnings with the legend of Moshup, their god and legendary whaleman. They believed the ashes from Moshup's pipe formed the islands.

During the summer, both islands are extremely congested. Bringing your car is not recommended, and reservations must be made months in advance. You may wish to visit the islands after Labor Day when the crowds have departed.

To Martha's Vineyard: Ferries sail from Woods Hole to Vineyard Haven (forty-five minutes) year-round. Contact the Steamship Authority at (508) 477-8600; www.island ferry.com.

During the summer months ferries sail into Oak Bluffs from Woods Hole or Hyannis. Contact the Steamship Authority or Hy-Line Cruises at www.hylinecruises.com.

To Nantucket: Ferries sail from Hyannis year-round. The "Fast Boat" cuts the two-and-a-half-hour trip to one hour but is more expensive. Contact the Steamship Authority or Hy-Line Cruises.

20 Long Point Wildlife Refuge Trail

The 632 acres of this preserve make it one of the largest on the Vineyard. Primarily dedicated to the protection of wildlife, only part of the preserve is open to the public. The trail explores wooded areas, thickets, and dunes along the shore of the Atlantic Ocean and is bordered by two saltwater ponds. Be sure to consult tide charts for easier walking during low tide.

Distance: 2.0-mile loop
Approximate hiking time: 1 hour
Difficulty: Moderate
Trail surface: Hard packed soil, soft sand
Best season: All seasons
Other trail users: None
Canine compatibility: No dogs allowed
Fees and permits: Mid-June to mid-September: trustees members and children free, parking fee for basic-level members, parking and entry fee for non-members; mid-September to mid-June: no fee
Schedule: Dawn to dusk
Map: USGS Tisbury Great Pond
Starting point: Deep Bottom Road or Hughes Thumb Road, West Tisbury
Trail contact: The Trustees of Reservations; www.thetrustees.org
Special considerations: Soft sand

Finding the trailhead: To reach the Long Point Wildlife Refuge from the ferry during the off-season, drive straight ahead to the stop sign and turn left onto Water Street. At the next stop sign, turn right onto South Main Street. Drive uphill (0.3 mile) to Vineyard Haven/Edgartown Road and turn left (west). Drive 2.3 miles to a blinking light. Turn right onto Airport Road. Follow Airport Road for 2.5 miles until it ends at Edgartown/West Tisbury Road. Turn right (west) on Edgartown/West Tisbury Road for 1.7 miles to Deep Bottom Road. The entrance is well marked; turn left (south) and follow the signs for 2.6 miles to the parking area.

During season: Follow the directions above to Edgartown/West Tisbury Road. Go west on the Edgartown/West Tisbury Road for 0.3 mile to Waldron's Bottom Road. Turn left (south) and drive for 1.2 miles to the end of the road. Turn left on Scrubby Neck Road and follow it 0.2 mile to Hughes Thumb Road. Turn right (south) through the gate and drive 1.25 miles to the parking area (follow the signs). GPS N41 21.254'/W070 38.295'

The Hike

The pine-oak forest opens to one of the best remaining examples of rare coastal sand plains grasslands, which stretch to magnificent dunes lining the Atlantic shoreline. From the edge of the woods, long, narrow ponds alternate with fingers of land to create a mix of fresh and brackish waters, salt marsh, and ocean shore. Tisbury Great Pond, with its exquisite white sand beach, is lovely, but requires water shoes for wading because of shell fragments.

Salt spray roses add dashes of pink to the waving grasses and a fragrant scent to the salty air. They attract butterflies and moths of many kinds. Little red-bellied snakes search the ground for earthworms or slugs, and harriers and red-tailed hawks hunt during the day.

Miles and Directions

0.0 An information kiosk marks the start of the trail, which is on the south side of the parking area. Head south and take the right fork. Walk out onto the heath. Cross the roadway. Crushed shells—the remnants of seagulls' dinners—lie on the trail. Tisbury Great Pond soon comes into view. The saltwater pond is naturally cleansed by the ocean washing over the dike.

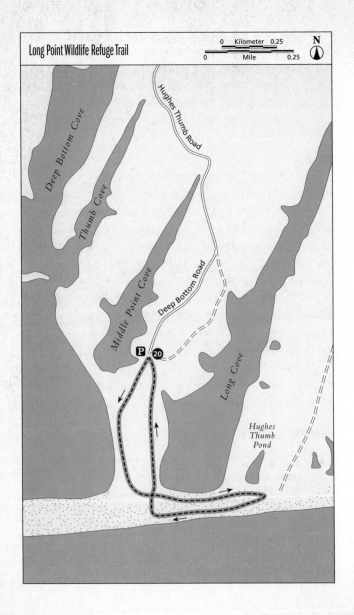

Long Point Wildlife Refuge Trail

0   Kilometer   0.25

0   Mile   0.25

N

Deep Bottom Cove

Thumb Cove

Middle Point Cove

Hughes Thumb Road

Deep Bottom Road

P 20

Long Cove

Hughes Thumb Pond

0.4 Cross the dunes to the beach. Enjoy the crashing waves as you walk along the shore. Watch for schools of dolphins that frequent the area.

0.7 Pass the first break in the dunes and enjoy the soft sand and extraordinary views.

1.0 Reach the second break in the dunes, then return down the beach and up over the dunes to the main trail. Walk a short distance back to the parking area.

2.0 Arrive back at the trailhead.

21 Menemsha Hills Reservation Trail

This trail winds through oak woodland and heath that cover the rolling hills sweeping up to the edge of great sand cliffs. Standing 150 feet above a stretch of rocky beach, the cliffs are one of the best places on the island to watch the sunset.

Distance: 3.5-mile lollipop
Approximate hiking time: 2 hours
Difficulty: Moderate/more challenging
Trail surface: Hard packed soil
Best season: All seasons
Other trail users: None
Canine compatibility: No dogs allowed

Fees and permits: Requested donation
Schedule: Dawn to dusk
Maps: USGS Naushon Island and Squibnocket
Starting point: North Road, Chilmark
Trail contact: The Trustees of Reservations; www.thetrustees .org
Special considerations: None

Finding the trailhead: To reach the Menemsha Hills Reservation from the ferry, drive straight ahead to the stop sign and turn left onto Water Street. At the next stop sign, turn right onto South Main Street. Drive uphill past Vineyard Haven/Edgartown Road. South Main Street becomes State Road in the outskirts of Vineyard Haven. At 2.4 miles, reach the intersection with Old County Road. Go right, continuing on State Road. At 2.6 miles, take the right fork onto North Road and drive west 4.7 miles to the entrance sign and parking area on the right. GPS N41 21.865'/W070 44.529'

The Hike

Beginning in the wooded parking lot, take a minute to check out the information kiosk showing the wide expanse of this reservation. As you begin making your way up the elevation, take note of the many views. Across Vineyard Sound, the Elizabeth Islands, Nobska Point, and the town of Falmouth are visible.

For more views of the island, climb to the top of Prospect Hill. The second highest point on the Vineyard, at 308 feet, it offers spectacular views of the village of Menemsha and Aquinnah beyond.

Harbor seals often bask on the beach and waterfowl are a common sight offshore. Deer call the woodlands home and red-tailed hawks hunt in the heath. This trail will challenge you with the greatest change in elevation of any trail on the Vineyard.

Miles and Directions

0.0 The trail begins at an information kiosk on the west side of the parking area. Take the left fork and wind into the deep woods of the Harris Trail Loop.

0.5 Complete the west side of the loop. Go uphill on the connecting path to the Upper Trail. At the top of the rise, turn left for the short detour to Prospect Hill. Return to the main trail and drop through a stand of oaks and across a dirt roadway.

0.9 At the trail intersection, turn left onto the Lower Scenic Trail, marked BEACH. The terrain is hilly; the trail switches back several times. Descend to an overlook with a magnificent view of the village of Menemsha and Menemsha Pond. Continue through an area of heath, crossing a plank bridge. Descend to a wooden bridge.

1.9 Lower Scenic Trail ends. Make a sharp left at the trail fork, following the yellow blazes. Walk 0.2 mile straight ahead to the Great Sand Cliffs Overlook and gaze out across Vineyard Sound. When you are ready, return to the main trail. **Option:**

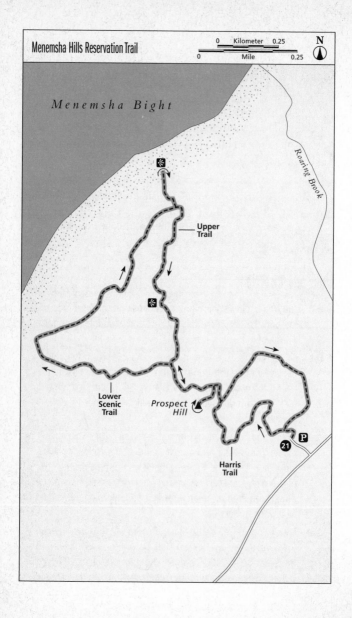

Menemsha Hills Reservation Trail

0   Kilometer   0.25

0   Mile   0.25

N

Menemsha Bight

Roaring Brook

Upper
Trail

Lower
Scenic
Trail

Prospect
Hill

Harris
Trail

P

21

From the Great Sand Cliffs Overlook, follow the trail cut into the steep cliff to the rocky shore below. The trail (0.6 mile round-trip) is difficult, but if you enjoy waves roaring onto rocks, the scenery is great, especially at high tide.

2.5 At the trail intersection, go straight (uphill) on the Upper Trail. The trail curves right, then joins the Lower Scenic Trail.

2.8 Follow the trail signs back across the road, through the wall and up the hill on the connecting trail. Pass the trail to Prospect Hill and descend to the top of the Harris Loop Trail.

3.2 Make a sharp left. Continue into the lowland (at rainy times it may be hard to pass) as the trail widens. Join the original trail, turn left, and return to your car.

3.5 Arrive back at the trailhead.

22 Tupancy Links

The trail at Tupancy Links allows you to walk to the bluff that rises from the sea along the north shore of Nantucket. Cliff Beach, 42 feet below (and inaccessible), is a narrow strip of sand gently washed with the softer waves of the sound. Easily accessible parking and open fields make this dog-welcoming trail a favorite with the locals.

Distance: 1.25-mile loop
Approximate hiking time: 30 minutes
Difficulty: Easy
Trail surface: Hard packed soil
Best season: All seasons
Other trail users: None
Canine compatibility: Dog friendly

Fees and permits: None
Schedule: Dawn to dusk
Map: USGS Nantucket
Starting point: Cliff Road, Nantucket
Trail contact: Nantucket Conservation Commission; www.nantucketconservation.org
Special considerations: None

Finding the trailhead: To reach Tupancy Links from the intersection of Broad Street and North Water Street, drive north on North Water Street in Nantucket Town for 0.2 mile to a three-way intersection. Continue straight ahead and then to the left onto Cliff Road, following Cliff Road west for 1.4 miles to the parking area on the right. GPS N41 17.328'/W070 07.570'

The Hike

As you enter the turnstile and head out in the wide open fields, it is easy to picture this once fertile farmland buzzing with animals and activity. Stroll through a meadow that was cleared in 1921 to create a golf course. The Nantucket Golf

Course expanded to eighteen holes, half of which were later donated to the Nantucket Conservation Foundation by Mr. and Mrs. Oswald A. Tupancy.

At the tip of the loop you will find an overlook that sits atop a very steep cliff. Bring the binoculars and rest on the bench to focus in on Dionis Beach, Eel Point, and Tuckernuck Island to the west. Look for Jetties Beach, the entrance to Nantucket Harbor, and the skyline of Nantucket Town against the eastern horizon. Several species of sea birds and ducks frolic in Nantucket Sound.

Nantucket was forested with tall oaks and pines when Europeans landed here in the seventeenth century. Early settlers cut trees for homes and ships. By 1779, Nantucket had been stripped of forest. For more than a hundred years, sheep grazed on the "Commons," as the moors are known locally. As the sheep declined, sweet pepperbush, highbush blueberry, bayberry, honeysuckle, and broom grew in the sandy soil. It was on this site that Nantucket shadbush was discovered. Originally believed to only exist on Nantucket, this variety of shadbush also grows on Long Island and the barrier beaches of New Jersey. Classified as a "special concern" species, this bush is also known as the juneberry or sugarplum.

Miles and Directions

0.0 Begin by walking through the turnstile; take the right fork uphill. The trail is a cart path, wide enough for partners to walk side by side. At the crest of the hill, you'll have a sweeping view of the rolling landscape. Actually dunes stabilized by grass, the short hills are fun to traverse to the first trail intersection.

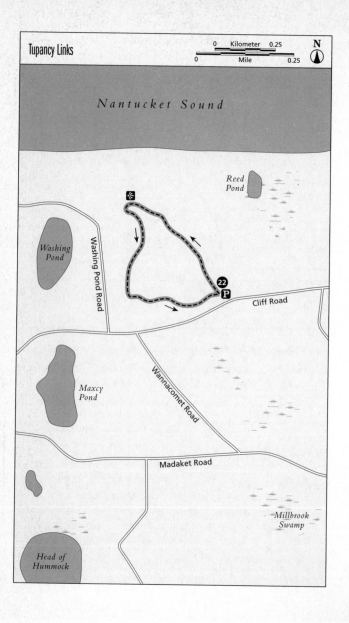

Tupancy Links

Nantucket Sound

Reed Pond

Washing Pond

Washing Pond Road

Maxcy Pond

Wannacomet Road

Cliff Road

Madaket Road

Millbrook Swamp

Head of Hummock

0   Kilometer   0.25
0   Mile   0.25

N

0.5 Turn right (north) and ascend to the bluffs through a carpet of bearberry, thickets of bayberry, and pasture rose. Reach the overlook. Do not cross the barrier fence to the cliff edge—it is very dangerous. Go back south to the trail intersection and bear right, heading west the narrow trail through the beach grass and heath plants. The trail winds near private property and connects to the cart-path loop. Continue straight on the cart path, south across the field to a trail intersection. Turn left onto the narrow trail and pass through a pitch pine grove to return to the parking area.

1.25 Arrive back at the trailhead.

23 Sanford Farm, Ram Pasture, and Woods Trail

This trail explores the southern half of Nantucket. The trail meanders through a beautiful, open field ending at a lush, secluded beach. This is a well-marked walk that teaches the agricultural roots of the island at each informational marker. The length of this hike is deceiving as you get swept up in the beauty of your surroundings.

Distance: 6.2 miles out and back with two loops
Approximate hiking time: 2.5 hours
Difficulty: Moderate
Trail surface: Hard packed soil
Best season: All seasons
Other trail users: None
Canine compatibility: Dog friendly

Fees and permits: None
Schedule: Dawn to dusk
Map: USGS Nantucket
Starting point: Madaket Road, Nantucket
Trail contact: Nantucket Conservation Commission; www.nantucketconservation.org
Special considerations: Heavy tick population

Finding the trailhead: To reach the Sanford Farm and Ram Pasture from Main Street, drive slowly for 0.7 mile on the cobbled street. You'll need the time to savor the sights anyway. At the Soldiers and Sailors Monument, take the right fork onto Upper Main Street for 0.3 mile. The road changes to brick before Caton Circle, which is an intersection of four roads with a flagpole in the center. Bear left (west) onto Madaket Road and drive west for 1.5 miles to the parking area on the left. GPS N41 17.006'/W070 08.210'

The Hike

Begin your walk across a lovely meadow, along the edge of Trots Swamp, a stretch of freshwater wetlands, and into a stand of pitch pines. On top of a rise, a wooden barn stands sentry over an incredible view. Hummock Pond glistens beyond the Ram Pasture, now dotted with osprey nest posts. Rolling dunes separate the two sections of the pond from the Atlantic beach.

Hummock Pond was one U-shaped pond until 1978. During a winter storm, the waves drove enough sand over the dunes to split the pond in two at its narrowest point. Today, the wetland habitat of the ponds attracts waterfowl.

Originally the peninsula, called Nanahuma's Neck for a popular sachem (native chief), was forested. The Sherburne Settlement was established by the English here in 1659. They called the strip surrounded by Hummock Pond Long Woods. Later, settlers felled the trees for pasture. Rams were contained with an elaborate series of high fences and ditches to control the time of year that lambs were born.

Miles and Directions

0.0   The trail begins next to the gate at the southeast side of the parking lot. Follow the dirt road straight south across Sanford Farm's cow pasture to the first trail intersection.

0.3   Stay straight past the first and second trail intersections (loop turnoff) and continue south toward the barn.

1.6   Reach the barn, which is a nice place to rest and enjoy the view. After your rest, walk south to the fork at the top of the beach loop. Turn right along the northern side of the pasture and come to a trail intersection. Turn left (south) off the

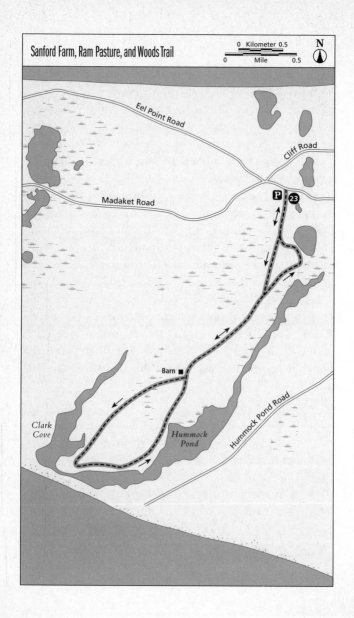

Sanford Farm, Ram Pasture, and Woods Trail

0   Kilometer   0.5

0   Mile   0.5

N

Eel Point Road

Cliff Road

Madaket Road

P 23

Barn

Clark Cove

Hummock Pond

Hummock Pond Road

roadway onto the narrow trail. Hummock Pond is on your right.

2.6 Pass the stile in the fence, then cross the dunes to the beach. Return to the pasture and follow the fence east toward the other section of Hummock Pond. The trail circles the east side of the pasture and rejoins the main trail.

4.2 From here, retrace your steps up past the barn and down into the wetlands to the base of the loop.

4.9 Take the right fork. Pass the head of Hummock Pond and Waqutaquaie Pond before rejoining the main trail.

5.9 Turn right to return to the parking area.

6.2 Arrive back at the trailhead.

About the Author

Pam VanDrimlen, a native of the Massachusetts South Shore, has lived on Cape Cod for twenty-one years. A mother of two and a small business owner, she loves hiking, biking, and kayaking, especially with her black Labrador, Macie. She hopes you enjoy the lovely places she discovered as much as she and her family have!